I Need a Man's Pants to Wash

I Need a Man's Pants to Wash

Lorie Kleiner Eckert

PELICAN PUBLISHING COMPANY
Gretna 2002

*The word "Pelican" and the depiction of a pelican are trademarks
of Pelican Publishing Company, Inc., and are registered
in the U.S. Patent and Trademark Office.*

Library of Congress Cataloging-in-Publication Data

Eckert, Lorie Kleiner.
  I need a man's pants to wash / Lorie Kleiner Eckert.
    p. cm.
  ISBN 1-58980-018-4 (pbk. : alk. paper)
    1. Divorced women—United States—Psychology. 2. Single
women—United States—Psychology. 3. Jewish women—
United States—Psychology. I. Title.

HQ834 .E26 2002
305.48'9652—dc21

                                  2001059805

Printed in Canada
Published by Pelican Publishing Company, Inc.
1000 Burmaster Street, Gretna, Louisiana 70053

In memory of my friends,
Lori Wacksman Martin
12/11/57-8/8/96
and
JoAnn Thompson Richardson
3/1/39-1/8/99

No one is guaranteed tomorrow.
We have no choice, therefore,
but to make the most of today.

Contents

Introduction

For a writer wanting to get into print, it was a surreal experience. I was trying to convince the publisher of my local Jewish newspaper to reprint an article I had written for another publication. Instead of agreeing to my idea, he suggested a different one—that I write a weekly column. This meant I'd get published fifty-two times instead of once! The publisher wanted the column slanted toward Jewish singles and I wanted to syndicate it nationwide. We agreed and shook hands, and I went home to write.

Quite frankly, I had no idea what would make a singles column Jewish. But then I thought about the Yiddish that all four of my grandparents spoke when I was a child. And I remembered the sadness I have felt that my children were not similarly exposed to it. Before long, I realized I could sprinkle my columns with that language and include a glossary at the end of each to define terms. Thus I got excited to think I could help a new generation enjoy Yiddish.

The next problem was what the main thrust of my writing would be. Since I was forty-eight years old at the time, a giggly column about guys did not seem appropriate. Instead I decided I would function as a cheerleader with the message: *I know you don't want to be alone, but I am sure that you can handle it.* Thus I began to encourage singles of all ages to be self-sufficient as I told the stories of my life and found the lessons within them. And of course, I giggled about guys on occasion.

I began to write these articles in March 2000 and this is a compilation of the first fifty-two of them. I am proud to report that this book contains 112 Yiddish words. All of them are italicized in the text and defined in a glossary at the end of the book. I am equally proud to report that my columns have appeared in twenty-one Jewish newspapers in America. In a funny postscript to this story, however, the publisher who suggested the columns in the first place has never printed any of them. Of course, I've had to get a little distance from this writing experience to find it amusing . . . which is just one more lesson I've learned—and now taught—through my columns.

Nu? Enough *kibitzing*, already. Read the book, *bubeleh!*

Alone

There was a burned-out light bulb high up in the garage and an outdoor spotlight that I had tried to change only to have the bulb break off in the socket. There was the door from the kitchen to the laundry room whose handle fell off—months ago—and let's not forget the miniblinds in the basement, which fell from the window whenever I adjusted or dusted them. My neighbor told me that when it rained water cascaded from the gutter by my kitchen window. He explained that the gutter needed cleaning, promised to clean it, but never did. And finally, there was a large piece of plywood up on my roof that blew there in last year's tornado.

Fortunately for me, my garage had two bulbs in its ceiling and one of them still burned, and the same was true for the outdoor spotlight. Additionally, I had learned to deal with the laundry-room door, which is to say I stopped closing it, and as for those miserable miniblinds, I cursed them with some regularity. I felt

sorry for the neighbors who had to look at that plywood on my roof, and I worried about the clogged
gutter, not to mention the fact that some day the
remaining bulb in the garage would burn out. And
then one day, the unthinkable happened. The door to
my shower stall broke, leaving me and it unhinged. I
had two choices—start taking baths or find a man, a
handy man, a man with tools.

Welcome to my world. I am a *gerushah,* a divorced
woman, and while it is true that I run my own business
and I am a Superwoman in many ways—I am faster
than a speeding bullet in creating *matzah*-ball soup for
a sick child and able to be at my parents' side in a single bound when they are ill—it is also true that I am a
complete failure with tools and a frightened *klutz* on
ladders. When my toilet gets stopped up I know to call
a plumber. When my house is overrun with bugs I know
to call an exterminator. But whom do I call with my
honey-do list?

There was that one plumber who told me over a
clogged drain that he was always available to do odd jobs
for single women. But when he mentioned as his only
"for instance" the need to turn my mattress, I felt a little
uncomfortable with his thought process. And so in my
time of need I turned to the handyman section of the
Yellow Pages, where I spotted several such businesses,
including the name of a house painter who had done
some work for me in the past. Knowing that he was reli-
able and not involved in rape, pillage, and plunder, I
called him. He came that very day with two helpers in
tow, and within fifteen minutes those three men and a
ladder had my house in order. I was thrilled, even after I

got the bill—and I won't tell you what it cost because you'd *plotz* and tell me that there was indeed some plunder involved—but the bottom line is that my to-do's are done and showering is once again an option.

Shortly after my experience, I received a long-distance call from my folks. They told of their tortured sleep the night before. Their smoke alarm had begun to beep repeatedly in the middle of the night, informing them of the need to replace the battery. Not as surefooted as they were in decades past, they decided to just listen to it and deal with finding and climbing a ladder the next day. And so with a steady beep . . . beep . . . beep . . . they passed the night. I laughed at their story and took solace from it too. For I had thought that my own story was not just one of minor inconveniences but instead the story of the sometimes-aching aloneness of divorce. It was nice to be reminded that more than fifty years of togetherness could not save my folks from similar feelings of helplessness, nor could it assuage their desire to be rescued from their predicament. I will try to remember that the next time I stand wet and naked in the shower embracing a cold and unhinged shower door and when it is my turn to hear things that go beep in the night.

I Need a Man's Pants to Wash

Let me give you a little background so that you will understand. Though I am definitely a Jew, my strongest allegiance to my faith is probably gastrointestinal. I hanker after *kugel, kasha,* and *knishes.* I also have a propensity to cry when movies portray Jewish weddings and funerals. And though I bless candles, wine, and *challah* during my *Shabbos* dinners, my spirituality is more in line with New Age thinking. I meditate each morning to a special mantra and put out positive messages to the universe in hopes of manifesting my dreams. I do this in spite of the "Psycho Dairy Farm" cartoon I read that showed a pig in meditation saying, "I can be kosher. I will be kosher. I am kosher." Additionally, I am forever in search of signs from the heavens that I am on the right track in life and thus I am pleased by all the lucky pennies I find along the way. I was thrilled, therefore, when I wrote my last book and found 165 coins in the process, and I was tickled by seventeen feathers that came my way, making my writing "fly." We New Agers don't believe in coincidence. Everything is *beshert.*

Another thing you need to know is that I adored my *bubbie,* and though she has been dead since 1993, I am still learning her lessons. One day, when I was newly married and she was eight years into widowhood, I asked why she never remarried. Her response was incomprehensible at the time, though I understand it after twenty-one years of marriage and a divorce. She said, "I need a man's pants to wash?" Over the years I have toyed with the idea of using her words in my creative endeavors. In the aftermath of divorce I have become a motivational speaker, fiber artist, and author. The lectures I give and the books I write are illustrated with my artwork, contemporary quilts with words and symbols pieced into the design. At the edge of my consciousness, I can visualize a quilt with rows of plaid boxer shorts, captioned with her comment.

The reason that I have not yet made the "Bubbie quilt" is that I don't know how to punctuate it. Do I use a question mark as Bubbie did to show disdain for marriage, or do I use a period to say I'm ready to sign on for another go? I have pondered these questions since my divorce and still have no answer. When I talk to audiences about getting in touch with their inner truth, I suggest that they try writing about their issues. Isn't it "coincidental," then, that the publisher of a Jewish newspaper invited me to begin writing a column about being single and Jewish?

OK, now try to understand. And while you do, remember that I don't believe in coincidence, because here's the second one and it's a little odd or perhaps totally strange. Today I was out for my daily walk and I found a dime in the street, and then I found a second something too. I found a pair of men's boxer shorts. At first I walked past them, but then I heard Bubbie's cryptic comment in my head and decided that I could not let them lie there. So I went back, picked them up, and carried them home, holding them at arm's length like a dead rat by the tail. They are now washing for the fifth time in scalding water and bleach, and I have likewise washed my hands with a fetish.

I can hear you wondering, "Is she *meshugeh?*" But what if it's a sign, a heavenly prod toward punctuating Bubbie's sentence? And so I will hold on to those shorts as I commence writing about being an "Attractive DJPF, 48, 5'7", 122 lb., mother of 3" and I will see where all of it takes me. I hope you will come along on the journey as I explore whether those boxer shorts are a symbol of what I no longer want (give me a break, they had brown streaks!) or if they are waiting here for some man to fill them (they're a size large—any takers?).

So now you understand and now I have begun and soon we will see what we see.

Cappuccino

Some women go to bars to meet men, but not me. I do most of my flirting over the cappuccino machine at my local gas station. I just love the stuff, and I am literally a card-carrying member of the gas-station coffee club, having my card punched after every purchase, getting every seventh cup free. There are a surprising number of men who drink this sweet stuff and I strike up a conversation with each one I meet. How often do they drink it? What's their favorite flavor? And do they promote it like an evangelist to their friends?

As for me, I drink one cup every Saturday and Sunday morning, and when I wrote my last book, the completion of each chapter was celebrated with a visit to the gas station. (All right, so there were twelve chapters and I got a "cuppa" two days in a row at the quarter, half, and three-quarter points, not to mention at the finish line.) My flavor of choice is hazelnut, but English toffee and French vanilla will do. And, yes, the manufacturer should pay me for all the promotion I give their product.

I have tried cappuccino in coffee shops but do not like it at all. It's too strong and costs a fortune, while the gas station only charges sixty-nine, seventy-nine, and eighty-nine cents for the twelve-, sixteen-, and twenty-ounce servings. Every now and again they have a special where any size cup costs sixty-nine cents and, ever conscious of getting my money's worth, I got addicted to twenty-ounce servings in this manner.

I figure I can learn a good deal about a man from his cappuccino habit. Right off the bat I know that since he's at the gas station and not the coffee shop he likes sweets and he's frugal. I also know that he probably lives in the area. If he tells his friends about his drinking habit he's a good sport, because he must surely take a ribbing. And I know about his addictive propensity by how much of it he drinks. Would I want to link my financial future to a man who is so out of control as to drink three of them a day—what if he gets introduced to casinos next?

Today is Sunday and so I stopped by my friendly neighborhood gas station to get my fill. No men were lingering but I met a wonderful woman there. She told me that if I make a one-time purchase of a special sixteen-ounce mug, I can fill it at each visit for only forty-nine cents. (And they will still punch my card!) We discussed that economically and calorically it's probably wise for me to do this. She also told me that every January the gas station picks a name out of a hat and that person gets free coffee for a year, and she's this year's winner. As if she's reading a Torah passage at the High Holidays, she tells me that this has been a blessing and a curse because now she drinks two cups a day!

As I walk from the gas station laughing, my thoughts get all mixed up—men, cappuccino, blessings, and curses—and when I rearrange the words in my mind I come up with this thought on my single status. It is a blessing to be single because I can drink as much of this stuff as I want without some man peering at me over the top of his glasses as he mutters, "You're going out for another cappuccino?" And of course, it's a curse to be alone, as there is no one with whom to toast my various successes over a cuppa brew. In my mind I hear the words of Deuteronomy—"I set before you today a blessing and a curse"—and I know the admonition is to "choose life and live it." I realize that I have chosen divorce and thus my current life, and now I must live it fully and happily, and I realize that in fact I do. And so I pat myself on the back for being able to find so much pleasure in such a small thing as cappuccino and over the fact that I remember to buy myself treats and celebrate my successes. I am so pleased to be having such wise thoughts that I consider going back to the gas station for more coffee. Life is wonderful. So is hazelnut cappuccino.

My Sin

I've always been a good girl in life—neat, sweet, and in my seat. Well, all right, there was that one time in high school when I had a party and we spilled lemonade on the carpet and scratched one of my brother's Temptations records, but I apologized, was forgiven, and never acted up again. It was shocking to everyone, therefore, when at the age of forty-two I took an enormous step off the expected path and got divorced. This really felt like quite a crime at the time, and in reality still does, as there is a pervasive myth in my family that divorce does not happen. Now, on my mom's side of the family this is fairly true, but my dad's side is another story altogether. Of nine first cousins, two have never married, one is in a long-term marriage, and the rest of us have been divorced at least once, not to mention my dad's brother who divorced a generation earlier. But in spite of all this history, the end of my marriage felt like an anomaly, a crime, a *shandeh*.

In the years since my divorce, these feelings have

enveloped me like cologne, and as I contemplate "my sin," I come to realize that those who wish to call me a sinner are looking at the wrong offense. My divorce is not what I did wrong in life, as there is a larger and perhaps even precipitating sin to consider. It is this— after two years of marriage, my then husband and I decided to leave our hometown of St. Louis and move to California. This move had all the sanctions of society as we were pursuing a new career for him and our share of the American Dream. But in reality we were breaking up a family—our extended family—as surely as would "the other woman." We were also putting a heavy and perhaps unbearable burden on our relationship, as we each became everything to the other in the absence of that most important thing, our *mishpoche.*

As I wax poetic over the concept of family, I will also confess that at the time I needed to leave St. Louis, as I was meshugeh from those very same people, who had a tendency to make demands upon my time, have great expectations of our relationship, and, in general, *hak mir a chainik.* After running away from my family, I learned a funny thing, however—friends do the same things. The only difference is that friends tend to come and go, whereas family is always "there" for you. Thus if a person must learn to deal with others, it seems a better investment of time, energy, and love to learn to deal with family.

Feeling as I do, it was odd for me when a friend boasted recently that her son was in Spain, loved it there, and might never return home. I was appalled at her news. Spain?! I know that they can be in constant touch via e-mail and the phone, but what comfort will that be when one of them is ill, when one of them has a car in the shop and needs a ride, or when one of them has a *simcha* to celebrate? My own personal Diaspora is not much better. My son has left home for graduate school in New York, my older daughter will follow in my footsteps and move to California upon college graduation, and my younger daughter aspires to either coast for college in a year. And what can I say to these beloved children as my heart screams on many levels—for my sake and for theirs—"Don't go!"? How do I have the *chutzpah* to tell them to do as I say not as I did? How do I explain that there's nothing out there in the great beyond that is more important than family? How do I do anything except let them move and learn their own lessons?

I was in St. Louis recently and had lunch with my aunt, who is ninety-one years old. She told me of her wonderful life while also making clear the fact that her life would be entirely different and better still if one of her two children—or even if I—lived in town. And I know she's right. And I know we have all missed out on a lot. And I know that this is my sin in life.

Code Word: Cookie

I found myself in the company of an amazing group of women. It was at a dinner party given by my friend, a stellar salesperson in a male-dominated industry, a woman who could always close the sale. Also present was our mutual friend, a highly successful stockbroker and financial columnist. And rounding out our high-powered half-dozen were an entrepreneur and two Ph.D.s. Of these three, one was a college professor and the other two worked in community development. Though I'm not sure what I expected that evening, I am quite sure it was not what I got, for what we women served up over dinner was a long conversation about men. Oh yes, for *forshpeiz* over wine, we got to know each other by briefly discussing our careers, and for dessert over a *glezel tai,* we debated the validity of astrology, but for the main course, we moaned and *kvetched* about men—how to find them, how to keep them, and what on earth it is that they want.

I don't wish to imply that I did not enjoy and participate fully in this conversation. It was informative to hear how these women juggled the polarities of being sexual but single adults, and it was a gas to giggle over the various escapades—make that sexcapades—of our sextet. My creativity was even sparked that evening as I suggested a garage sale of sorts where the six of us would recycle the "used" men of our lives, allowing one woman's castoff to be another woman's find. This plan fizzled, however, after I showcased the first man and it appeared that he was the ex-husband of the professor. Things were a bit tense—territorially speaking—until we determined that he was not, though he turned out to be the ex-husband of her friend!

But I guess having my creativity sparked was exactly what I had hoped for that evening; I just thought it would be on a professional level. I wanted each woman to tell me about her career and *kvell* about her accomplishments, so that I could glean bits of wisdom from her experience and be encouraged by her successes to aspire to more of my own. I wanted to hear of the glamorous aspects of her job as well as its ugly underbelly, so that I could return to my office ready to face the challenges of my own profession. In short, I wanted to be empowered by the lives of these women and feel full to overflowing with mine. Instead, I ached and felt empty, as we seemed to narrowly define a woman's success in life by the presence or absence of a man. As a sad case in point, one of the women had recently taken a year's sabbatical to write a first novel. The resultant manuscript was picked up by an agent, who then sold it to a major New York publishing company. Even with a sizeable advance firmly in hand, this woman only casually mentioned the experience, gave herself little credit for it, and instead found herself somehow lacking because she was alone.

In the early days of my divorce, I guess I agreed with this assessment. I was dating a man who was not very accessible, as he was frequently—all right, perpetually—out of town. As I ached over our relationship, I described it this way: "I was the round of dough and he the cookie cut from it. When we were together, he fit back perfectly into my empty space. I was complete and he was encircled by my love." It was a beautiful and romantic notion at the time, though it makes me quite nauseous, now as I refuse to see myself as incomplete and empty without a man. Sure I still want a relationship with a perfect fit, but that means a guy cut from the same dough, not from my hunk of it—a Gingerbread Joe to my Gingerbread Jane.

I am sure that I will spend many more evenings in the company of single women and that we will spend some of our time moaning about men. But as we do, I hope "Code Word: Cookie" will pop to mind and I will think of myself as Gingerbread Jane, whole, fully formed, and enhanced with lots of icing and candies, my many accomplishments. In that manner I will feel full to overflowing and empowered by my life.

A Tale of Two Professors

Last summer I dated a college professor who was a world-renowned authority in his field. I was completely turned on by his mind, not to mention—*gotenyu*—his hands. Ours was a torrid relationship that burned out in two months' time, and what I learned from the experience was that a fire that burns hot burns fast and then, poof, it goes out.

I had a little chat with God at the time and told Him I really needed to try that experience again, but I asked Him if the next man and I could take things a little more slowly, recognizing that perhaps it is wise to wait beyond the second date to get so physical. God must have laughed as He answered my prayer, and He must have muttered under his breath as well, "Be careful what you pray for."

It's months later and college professor number two has entered my life. He is a brilliant man whose many areas of intelligence do not overlap with my own, a man with whom I may have nothing in common but to whom I am attracted nonetheless. Go figure. He looks like Robert Downey, Jr., from the front and like Neil Diamond from the side, and I think both of these men are darling—well, all right, so all three of them are. It's very odd, but I am intrigued by the professor's clean-shaven face and the promise of a beard that is there, and I have a burning desire to watch him shave. I should also mention that he has a scar on his forehead, another by his eye, and a third on his chin, and they call out to me across restaurant tables—I want to touch them or kiss them or more.

Lest you worry about my *tsatske* status, let me mention that the man is a classic and cautious Capricorn, and as such he needs to be very certain before he gets involved in a relationship. The translation of this is that we have had four dates and he has yet to kiss me good-night. God laughs at His little game of *gantz* or *gornisht* while I am live wired with sexual *shpilkes*.

Our next date is Sunday night and I have visions of walking into his apartment, dropping to my knees, and begging him for a kiss. Another option I explore is appealing to his engineer's mind with my own funky math, explaining to him that with a combined age of ninety-six we may not have a lot of time to waste. The final alternative is to take a deep breath and wait for him to shock and excite me with a kiss in his own good time. I'll probably take that last option because of a little fantasy that plays in my head: I see Mr. Capricorn and myself in one of our gentle hugs and then I see him pull back from it a bit as he gazes into my eyes. His gaze is long and deep like the one he surprised me with over dessert the last time we were together. In the fantasy he informs me with great seriousness that he wants to kiss me, and I tell him that I would like it if he did. We hold each other's eyes until he lowers his face to kiss my forehead. I feel some consternation, but I just keep looking into his eyes until finally he tries it again, this time landing a kiss on my lips, the kiss of a brother. I don't know what to do, so I just look into his eyes until he bends a little farther than before and kisses me ever so gently on the side of my neck, at which time we continue our gaze and our eyes say more than lips ever could.

I find the fantasy to be ever so beautiful. So maybe I'll take that deep breath, remain calm as I recognize the steps we've taken—a hug here, an arm to hold there, that unexpected gaze over dessert—and try to be appreciative of the care he is giving our friendship and the respect he is giving me as a woman. And as I wait for our big moment, I know one thing for sure. There is definitely a lesson to be learned from this professor and from my ever-present and often comical God.

Thelma and Louise

It occurs to me that house hunting and shopping for a man are similar activities and that in both cases it is helpful to remember the wisdom of the famous movie characters, Thelma and Louise, who taught us that you get what you settle for.

I remember shopping for a home and thinking how much I loved the yard at house number one and how exquisite the master bedroom was in house number two and how workable the kitchen was in house number three and how much I always wanted a walkout basement like house number four. I also remember feeling discouraged when no one house possessed all of those elements—not to mention the fact that house number one was in the wrong school district and house number two was too expensive and house number three was on a busy street while house number four's walkout basement leaked.

In the case of homeownership, there is the possibility of building the dream house, but that's not possible in the search for a man. Therefore, though I have a list of all the male amenities I desire, I don't know how to proceed. All I know is that I want a man I can laugh with like boyfriend number one, a man so friendly and easy to *shmooze* with that I can imagine him belly laughing and backslapping with my kids as they discuss topics of every kind. I also want a man who loves to read like boyfriend number two, a man with a vast library of books that he has actually read, a man whose library overlaps with mine. My dream man must be spiritual like the guy who was behind my personal door number three, and if he could have the exact same amount of body hair, that would be sensuous indeed. And while we're on the topic, I want a man like boyfriend number four, a man so sexy that he removed the starch from my spine if he so much as looked at me, touched me, or got close enough to smell. And oddly, I also want a man like that guy I was married to, a solid citizen, a *mensch*, a man with some *gelt* in hand.

These are the cornerstones of the man I would build if male mortar and brick were available to me. But they are not, so I feel discouraged that thus far no one man has possessed all of these elements—not to mention the fact that boyfriend number one was a womanizer and boyfriend number two was not pleased that I had children and boyfriend number three was jealous and possessive and boyfriend number four was too fond of *shnaps* and a womanizer to boot.

The odd thing about the men I have dated is that I have often known from the start that they were not right for me, that something major was missing, and still I entered into the relationship, extending the benefit of the doubt. On the one hand, there is some wisdom to this approach, as it allows me to get to know men who are different from me and who may have entirely new things to teach me. On the other hand, however, I know this can be folly. I am reminded of a comment my daughter made about single adults in my age group. She said that we are all "some degree of desperate." I know that this often describes me. There are times when the only real requirement I have of a man is that he has the defining male amenity and is still breathing.

I am thinking back to my first house-hunting experience. I remember telling the realtor that the only mandatory feature for my starter home was a fireplace, and the first house she took me to did not have one. As she stood in the living room telling me that I could easily add a potbellied stove, my mind shouted, "But that's not what I want!" And so I replaced that realtor with one named Thelma, or was it Louise, and proceeded to hunt until I found a home that suited me and that I loved. As I continue my search for a man, I hope to remember the experience. For in both of these shopping expeditions, a person does indeed get what they settle for, and in both cases the matter is far too significant to just settle.

From Car Wrecks to Car Washes

I was in the fast lane of the interstate, traveling at my standard four miles over the speed limit, when, *mit'n derinnen,* a deer crossed my path. I had no choice but to hit it. Except for the fact that the collision caused my hood to pop all the way open, it may not have occurred to me to stop. But traveling at 69 miles per hour with zero visibility seemed unwise, so I pulled onto the median. At that time I noticed a lot of smoke coming from my car, feared an explosion, and ran from the vehicle. That's how I came to find myself standing in the dark, in the middle of the divided highway, with hundreds of cars whizzing by. To make matters worse, I was 200 miles from home.

Almost immediately, a man pulled his truck onto the shoulder of the slow lane, ran across three lanes of traffic, and asked me if there was anything I needed. I answered quite honestly, "I need a hug." And so he hugged me, ran back across those lanes of traffic, got into his truck—right beside his wife or girlfriend—and drove away. Luckily for me, a second man stopped to offer *rachmones* and, exhibiting a bit more *saichel*, I asked him to call AAA.

Some may fault me for getting off to such a slow start in handling this situation, but I don't. Perhaps I was in shock or just *tsemisht* as usual; it matters not. All that counts is that I eventually got my act together and did all that needed to be done. In this case, I dealt with the police, AAA, a tow truck, my insurance company, and, for weeks after, the body shop. In the old days, my husband would have dealt with all of these matters. But this incident took place soon after I became single and there was no husband to lean on, so I did it all myself. The payoff was increased self-esteem for being able to manage alone.

I like to believe that with each incident of this type, I earn a feather in my cap as a self-sufficient human being. In my years as a singleton, I have had the opportunity to earn a lot of them, doing a vast number of things that in the past would have been left to that husband. My list of successes includes items from the sublime to the ridiculous, and with pride I list a few. I have learned to pump gas and drive my car through the car wash. I have learned to make my own airline, hotel, and car-rental reservations. I have learned to find the airport's long-term parking lot, the shuttle bus, and my parked car a week later. I have learned to carry a suitcase that weighs half of what I do. I have learned how to negotiate major purchases and have bought a house, a new roof for that house, and not one but two water heaters (don't ask). I not only bought a new car but I ran an ad in the newspaper and sold an old one as well. I have so many feathers in my cap at this point that it is beginning to look like a full-plumed Indian headdress, and I am proud of my capabilities, my accomplishments, and myself.

I don't wish to imply that all of these successes came off without a hitch, but I do wish to say that the glitches don't count, only the ultimate achievements. When I purchased my home, for instance, the realtor asked casually after the closing if I had switched the utilities to my name and if I had let my insurance agent know when to begin coverage. He was shocked to learn that I had not and I was shocked to realize that I should have. But instead of wasting time calling myself a *dumkop*, I just made those calls and handled the situation.

If you ask me if I want to do all these things unassisted, I'd have to say no. And if you ask me if I prefer to be alone, I'd have to say no again. But if you ask me if I can handle doing these things alone, I'd have no choice but to proudly shout, "You bet!" From car wrecks to car washes, I can manage alone.

A Modern-Day Verse for Ecclesiastes

My daughter Shana graduated from college last Sunday and I don't know what to wish for her. Oh yes, I wish her happiness and peace and all those good things, but I'm talking about the foundation upon which that will be built, the role she chooses to play in life. A very large part of me wishes her the traditional female role. I want her to have a husband and a home and children and I want her to be able to focus on them exclusively. Another part of me wishes her a feminist version of life, with a meaningful career and the personal empowerment and high self-esteem that it can bring. And then the sum total of me *shreis gevalt* over the fact that a whole generation of women has been unable to figure out a hybrid of these two roles that can work.

This issue has plagued me since Shana's childhood, when I lived my life as a full-time wife and mother. During those years, my friend Lucy used to yell at me with some regularity, "What kind of example are you

setting for your daughters?!" I know that as a flag
bearer for feminism I was a huge failure, but then,
that wasn't the example I was trying to set. I was trying
to be a world-class *baleboosteh*. And I must state
emphatically that I think this is a vitally important role
to play. I hate to run on a platform of family values,
but really, is there anything more important? Beyond
the fact that children need a parent at home to offer
time of a qualitative and quantitative nature, a family
is a small business and needs someone to run it. But
as good as it is for the household and the children for
the mother to be home, this role can definitely be lim-
iting for the mother. So how do I espouse it for my
beloved child?

I have learned a lot in my midlife stint as a single
woman in pursuit of a career, and it's knowledge that I
want Shana to have. I have learned that there is a lot of
self-esteem to be earned along with a wage. I have
learned that when I am paid for my work I realize that
it has value. And most important I have learned that I
am capable of taking care of myself and all of my
needs. In my old life as a homemaker, I was like the
Little Engine of kiddie-literature fame. I walked
around saying, "I think I can, I think I can," without
ever proving to myself that I could. My career has
allowed me to prove the fact. It has shown me that
there are areas in which I can be a *mavin* and a *macher*
and this knowledge has empowered me. Additionally,
while the world pays lip service to the importance of
motherhood, the business world pays in cash, and like
it or not, cash is empowering too. I want all of these
perks for my daughter.

Perhaps my problems with the baleboosteh business were brought on by the fact that I never really explored other options before entering into it. For the first twenty-one years of my life I was a child in my father's home, and for the next twenty-one years I was a wife in my husband's. I was always dependent on a man. I never took time off between being a daughter and a wife to become that very important thing—a self-sufficient person. So maybe the traditional female role was not the problem, only my timing, and maybe I just need to wish Shana a period of self-discovery in the feminist world before she makes further decisions.

In Ecclesiastes, we learn that there is a season for everything and a time for every experience under heaven. And so this is what I wish for my daughter as she graduates from college: a modern-day verse for Ecclesiastes. I wish her a time for personal growth and then a time for nurturing the growth of others. I wish her a time to be single and self-sufficient and then a time to be part of a pair. In this manner I hope she will find personal empowerment, a strong foundation for happiness and peace in whatever role she chooses to play in life. And to this I say amen.

Journal Entry

I attended a singles dance tonight, all by myself, on the other side of town. It seemed safe, as if no one would know me and I wouldn't have to feel embarrassed. Once inside the door, I didn't know what to do with myself. Instantly, my arms crossed themselves against my chest, and as I uncrossed them I whispered, "Take a deep breath. Don't freeze. You can do this." I yelled at myself for not thinking of a game plan in advance, but I had not, so I just turned and spoke to the man standing beside me. I asked him a bunch of questions about the group. When I asked one he couldn't answer he turned me over to the next guy, who knew the answer, stated it, and then went on to tell me about his continuing difficulties with alcoholism and his participation in AA. I scratched that candidate from the list.

Two or three men over, there was a handsome man, the kind I would choose if I were a woman who could say, "You, I want you." When it came to pass that we began talking and dancing, I uttered a little prayer of gratitude. Unfortunately, as we spoke I learned he wasn't one I could bring home to mother. He was from a different world and educational level, and though socioeconomic levels shouldn't matter, they do. But how could I have known by looking at him? Before I knew it, he was buying me a soda and I felt beholden to him, which was OK because there really was no one else I was interested in—well, there was that one guy who was sexy but not tall enough and that other guy who was really built but already taken. Thus it was OK to spend time with this man. But then, while he was at the bar buying me that sixty-five-cent Sprite, another interesting guy entered the room, walked right over to me, and asked me to dance. Unsure of the rules, I said yes.

It's funny what a difference there can be in two dancers. This one was shorter and thus more comfortable to embrace, and he held me in a more confident manner. He was also easier to talk to and his career was more in line with the people with whom I normally associate. After dancing to two songs, though, I began to feel funny about the tall man, so I went back to him and my waiting Sprite.

When the time approached for me to leave, I tried to figure out a way to slip my card to dancer number two but couldn't think of one. So I made a point of leaving very slowly, hoping he'd catch my act, and then I loitered outside hoping he'd follow me. When he didn't, I thought of staking out the place until he left but decided against it. I have a little regret that such a good prospect got away. I wonder if he was my true love—lost before he was found—and I comfort myself with the thought that if he had ten more minutes to talk to me he would have told me about his addiction too.

As I reflect on the evening, I think of a girlfriend who said she made a fool of herself at a singles event by making out with some man. I wonder who on earth she might have chosen in the crowd I was in. And I cringe to think that there was a time in the early days of my singleness when I would have been kissing someone too, or worse yet, when I would have thought I had found my true love in someone there, anyone there, just so I wouldn't have to be alone.

I had been afraid to go tonight, afraid it would be completely awful and leave me depressed for days. Instead, it was only slightly awful and leaves me feeling empty. I try to fill that emptiness with pride in myself for going there, staying there, and managing to talk to two men who interested me. I'm thinking there must be some sort of art to these events so that you can move easily from man to man. But even though I had a basically OK time, I'll hope not to go back and learn.

When I got home I took a really long and hot shower. I feel better now. Oh, what a night.

Love Lessons Cinema Style

❦

Hooray for Hollywood and its varied offerings—today I'll review three movies. On screen one we have the 1989 classic *When Harry Met Sally,* featuring Billy Crystal and Meg Ryan. On screen two we have the 2000 film *28 Days,* starring Sandra Bullock. And on screen three we have the 1996 movie, *The Mirror Has Two Faces,* starring Barbra Streisand and Jeff Bridges. Good movies all, all with lessons to teach us.

Beginning our movie marathon is *When Harry Met Sally.* Male and female relationships are the focus of this film, which asks the question, can men and women be friends? Time and again, the dialogue answers the question in the negative while movie scenes show just the reverse, as we watch the slow growth—over more than a decade—of deep friendship between Harry and Sally. Eventually sex gets in the way of their friendship when it enters the relationship before both partners are ready to make a commitment. They part ways only to realize in their solitude how well they know, like, and love each other and how central their friendship is to their lives—in spite of or maybe even because of their many quirks. As Harry tells Sally when they reconcile, "I love that you get cold when it's seventy-one degrees out. I love that it takes you an hour and a half to order a sandwich. I love that you get a little crinkle in your nose when you're looking at me like I'm nuts . . . and I love that you are the last person I want to talk to before I go to sleep at night." By movie's end their friendship turns to marriage, and the viewer leaves the theater laughing, cheering, and believing that such a love— based on an old friendship—can exist, survive, and thrive.

Sandra Bullock's movie is a different sort of "love story." She plays the part of a young woman who is addicted to alcohol and drugs and who is court ordered to attend a rehab program for twenty-eight days. Her goal, then, is to love herself enough to become clean and sober. A variety of group-therapy sessions is shown in the film and in one, a fellow patient asks the counselor how soon after leaving rehab it is safe to enter into a romantic relationship. He is told that in the first year he should buy a plant, in the second year he should buy a pet, and in the third year, if both the plant and the pet are still alive, then he should think about a relationship. This scene about *gedult,* giving things time, was worth the price of admission and I believe its message is applicable to many folks desirous of a romantic relationship—from young adults to the newly divorced or widowed. We all need time to stand alone first. And even then, when we find the head-over-heels love of which we dream, it's probably best to let that relationship settle for a while, let it stand the test of time, before rushing into a permanent arrangement.

Closing out our triple-dip movie date is Barbra Streisand in the role of a professor at Columbia University. Her character is painted as a plain Jane. Though professionally she is dynamic and successful, this power does not carry over to her personal life. As the movie opens, we find her in an unexciting relationship with a Woody Allen type of guy, a *nebbish,* a *mees* man. Of course by movie's end she is transformed from an ugly duckling to a beautiful swan and she wins the love of the handsome Jeff Bridges, but that's not the story line that intrigued me. Instead, I liked the mees man's story, for he too was transformed by closing credits when he found a woman to love. Strangely and comically, the woman looked just like him, and because they were a matched set inside and out, viewers watched two unattractive halves come together to become a beautiful, radiant, and enviable whole.

Perhaps it is odd to find real-life lessons in the fantasies of Hollywood, but I do, and here they are. Live life fully and keep your eyes open for your *besherter* right there in the midst of all that fullness. Remember always that love takes time. And never despair of finding love, because every pot has a lid.

Zipple.com

The desire to get rich quick is common in America. We dream of finding some relic in the attic that turns out to be a priceless antique, we line up to buy lottery tickets with regularity, and we think a time or two about the latest pyramid scheme that an acquaintance advances. And then, after a few minutes in the fantasy world, most of us chuckle at the lousy odds of getting rich in any of these ways and go back to our nine-to-five jobs. Similarly, in the world of being single, we sometimes hanker after a quick road to romance, and we dream of finding our true love in the two dozen personal ads in our city magazine or on that matchmaking Web site we stumbled across when we typed the word *lonely* into our favorite search engine last Saturday night. Though all of us know someone who has found true love in such a manner, it's still a long shot, and we should chuckle over such wishful thinking and get back to the real world. We really should do that, but for today let's not. Instead, let's explore the world of

Zipple.com, a Jewish personals database opened in July 1999 and discovered by me . . . well, last Saturday night. Though it purports to be "a comprehensive guide to Judaism on the net," I pushed past all the Jewish books, music, and educational resources and headed for the men in an area called "The Scene." There I became a new member and began the free registration process.

First I filled out a search criteria form. On it, I listed the age range of my dream man and the type of relationship I was looking for. Eight possibilities were listed, from e-mail buddies to marriage, and I clicked all that applied. I also had fifteen religious affiliations to consider. Every brand of Jew was there, from Reform to Hassidic to Jew by Choice. Oddly, I could also choose Catholic, Protestant, or Muslim, as Zipple is evidently an equal-opportunity matchmaker. After answering a few more questions I was asked the country, state, or area code in which I wanted to conduct my search. I chose the state of Ohio, punched the "search" button, and twenty-three male profiles filled my screen.

Each profile was three screens long. Screen one gave a Zipple name, city, marital status, height, body build, and a photo when available. If the guy was tall enough and lived close enough, I moved to screen two, which gave his hair and eye color, his level of physical activity and preferred sport, the industry in which he worked, his educational focus, the types of reading materials, movies, music, and restaurants he enjoyed, and the like. When I later filled out my own profile, I learned that all this information was gleaned from multiple-choice and fill-in-the-blank questions. Thus, when he told about his personality traits, he had had more than a hundred descriptive words from which to choose, from *artistic* to *open-minded* to *witty.* If he still sounded good after all those words, I could click onto the final screen, in which I got his answers to four essay questions. Here he told more about himself and stated his idea of the perfect woman, date, and relationship, each essay in thirty words or less.

Though at first blush I was intrigued by Zipple, I came to see that it had two major drawbacks. First, though it was exciting to have twenty-three names pop up on my screen, I soon realized that for men between the ages of forty-three and fifty-eight in the entire state of Ohio, this was a miniscule number. Second, when I read through the tall-enough/lives-close-enough profiles, of which there were six, I saw that five of the six were of such a get-rich-quick/instant-gratification mentality that they didn't even take the time to answer the essay questions. Indeed, some of them didn't even answer all the multiple-choice questions, making me wonder how much time they would be willing to devote to making a relationship work. Because of these drawbacks, I found Zipple to be like treading water—it occupied my time but it got me nowhere. And until the likes of Bill Gates turn the site into a monopoly of Jewish singles, I probably will not revisit it. Of course, I may change my mind if that one tall-enough/lives-close-enough/essay-writing man in Dayton writes me back sometime soon. . . .

Watering Woes

I have learned that most of my problems in life are solvable. The tricky part is recognizing that I've got a problem. A case in point is the story of my long struggle with the garden hose.

For me, one of the hardest things about becoming single was watering the lawn. I had been in a twenty-year marriage to a guy who took care of all outdoor things, so literally from the first day I moved into my house this chore was a challenge. While I live in a subdivision in which most landscaping concerns are taken care of by the homeowners' association, this did not include watering. Thus on that first day I found a note on my door telling me that a chemical treatment had been applied to my lawn that mandated I water it within twenty-four hours. I dutifully shuffled off to Wal-Mart to buy a hose and came back home to hook it up, only to learn that the previous owner had the odd habit of removing the handle from his outdoor spout so no one would use his water. I somehow found the handle, but I never found the screw that attached it. I owned exactly two screws, and the lady next door had about a dozen, but of course none of them fit.

After literally getting a handle on that situation, I proceeded to have a couple of years of fun with the fact that there was only one outdoor spout and it was in the back of the house. In order to water the front, I had to buy another hose to attach to the first one and drag it from the back to the front. This mass of hoses was unsightly, unwieldy, and forever knotted, causing me to buy a contraption to keep it neatly wound up. Suffice it to say that my new toy came unassembled.

While I am hardly an expert on hose racks, I am certain that the one I bought had a serious design flaw. The hose itself screwed into the cart, and then a little connector hose (a foot or two long) hooked the cart to the waterspout. Even after I bought a wrench to tighten all my connections, they never stayed tight. Thus I'd come out after thinking I'd been running the sprinkler on the front lawn for an hour only to learn that my connections had come undone, and all I had managed to do was flood the little area around the backyard spout instead. Trust me, it was frustrating.

My neighbor Steve came along then and suggested I hire a plumber to put a new spout in at the front of the house. What an idea! This allowed me to uncouple the *l-o-n-g* hose and keep more manageable hose lengths front and rear without the need for a cart. Of course, even these shorter hoses knotted on occasion and I bruised and muddied myself dealing with them, but it was a great improvement.

A Midwest fall came, and there was winter and there

was spring once again. I sat on my back porch regaling my friend Jet with all my many hose stories and worries. He laughed at my little comedy routine and then coaxed me to try again. "How hard can it be?" he said. "The hose is still connected to the spout. Just go turn it on." So I did. And we could hear water running. But nothing ever came out of the hose. Upon investigation, we discovered that the water pipe had burst over the winter, and by turning on the faucet, I had been watering the inside of my son's bedroom. It was then that I realized that I am powerless over lawn watering.

We all have nuisances in our lives about which we complain, and sometimes we even take pleasure in our complaining or derive some other benefit from it. But then it may happen that the nuisance crosses over a line to become a full-fledged problem. Personally, I know this has occurred when I feel the need to run away from home or totally demolish something. The upside to reaching this point is that as soon as I recognize I have a problem, I can go on to solve it. In the case of the garden hose, bids were solicited and received and an automatic sprinkler system was installed posthaste, allowing me to say with glee that I've sprinkled happily ever after.

Will I Know?

In the Broadway musical *Guys and Dolls,* Sr. Sarah Brown is a sergeant at the Save-a-Soul Mission and Sky Masterson is a gambler. To win a $1,000 bet he needs to convince her to go to Havana with him, and he does so by promising to provide her with something she needs—sinners for the Mission. One of the things they talk about in their time together is love, and in song each tells the other, "I'll know when my love comes along. I'll know then and there." And with this instant knowing that they both possess, they then proceed to fall in love with each other, a love-at-first-sight sort of thing.

Such an instant recognition of love is an interesting concept but not one that I expect for myself, as I have a tendency to be dense in all areas of my life. I once sat on my porch step in early spring and marveled at the hundreds of beautiful winged insects that suddenly came into view. It was quite shocking when my mother came outside minutes later and started *shrei'en* about termites swarming. And of course there was my first pregnancy, when I began having bad cramps at thirty-seven weeks of gestation and wanted to put myself to bed with the flu. I was truly anticipating diarrhea and was surprised to have a child instead.

I would be embarrassed to mention these incidents except that I know I'm not alone in my density. A good friend of mine, a man I dated for four years, was once feeling under the weather, and so he sat himself down in a recliner at home and tried for a couple of days to rest and nurse himself back to good health. When that didn't work, he took himself to a chiropractor who, upon examining him, insisted he go to a hospital. It was when my friend announced his intent to walk to the hospital that the chiropractor announced his suspicion that my friend was having a heart attack—a diagnosis that turned out to be correct.

I don't know who is dense and who denser, but don't expect the likes of us to go around singing, "I'll Know," because we won't. We'll need to *daven* over a book of instructions to find our way to true love, and that's exactly what I found in Richard Bach's 1984 book, *The Bridge Across Forever.* In it, the example of his life gives a recipe for such a search. For years he ran around dating woman after woman in search of his soul mate. During the process he played chess regularly with Leslie Parrish, a female friend to whom he confided all his dating escapades. It was many years into their friendship that he happened to look up over the chessboard and discover that she was *the one.*

I like this model of slow knowing and, quite frankly, I trust it more too. We've all heard stories of first dates in which the guy says to the girl, "You're the one I'm going to marry." Whether this is love at first sight or merely a guy who is too lazy to date around a bit is anyone's guess, but I'd be much more comfortable hearing those words after three months together than after three hours. Love isn't all magic—it's something that has to be worked at, and played at too. As a sad reminder of this fact, I need to report that the long-term marriage of Richard Bach and his soul mate, Leslie, recently ended in divorce.

So what can be said to all of these lovers, to Sister Sarah and Sky, to Richard and Leslie, to the Termite Infested and the Heart Attack Happening, to the instant knowers, the slow knowers, and the may-never-figure-it-outs? Perhaps it is this—beware! Recognition is the easy part, and then comes the challenge of making it work.

It is said of opportunity that people do not recognize it when it comes knocking at the door, because it comes dressed in overalls looking like work. I think the same may be said of love. This view is certainly not as romantic as humming a few bars of "I'll Know," but it is reality. Just think of Sister Sarah and Sky. It will certainly take a lot of effort to mix equal parts of saint and sinner into one serving of happily ever after.

Ich vais; this much I know.

Male Order

There's a certain allure to mail-order catalogs. The ease of shopping from the comfort of my home without having to drive to the mall, fight for a parking place, or *shlep* from store to store makes me try it time and again. It's easy to forget that even when I go to my favorite store and take five pairs of *hoizen* in the same size and style to the dressing room, only one pair will fit. And it's easy to forget the quantity of shoes in my size that I must try on before I find a pair narrow enough for my feet. Instead of my remembering these things, hope springs eternal and I place my catalog order, thinking that that one pair of jeans or shoes will be right for me. I am greatly disappointed, then, when my purchase arrives and pinches in the crotch or instep. I'm a little fretful too, because I know that as I return it, I will have to face William, the clerk at my local post office. He will take one look at that company's name, shake his head in disgust, and tell me again—as he has in months and years past—that he won't allow his wife to purchase mail-order goods because the only winner in the system is the U.S. Mail.

I'm embarrassed to admit it, but the same mentality that draws me to the mail-order catalogs also draws me to the personal ads. Instead of going to a singles event I like the ease of "shopping" from the comfort of my home without having to get *farputzt,* worry about the zit on my forehead, or *shvitz* over the fear of approaching a man. With all these perks in place, it is easy to forget that a man who sounds good in a thirty-word description may still be lacking. He may be tall, handsome, successful, and educated but not compassionate and spiritual, or he may be all of those things combined but still lack that spark. Still, hope springs eternal, and I write responses to ads.

The logical side of my brain tells me that both sorts of "catalog shopping" are nonsensical. As difficult as it is to choose a product by its photograph in the one case, in the other, we're not even shown a photograph, and as we rely on the man's words of description, we come to see that often they do not closely resemble the man. I remember the one "blond" guy who clearly had not noticed his hair color since he was a towhead at two. How could he not know his hair had turned brown? Then there was the guy who said he had a great sense of humor, but he never cracked a smile. And the worst for me—a female who has felt like an Amazon since she reached 5'7" at the age of eleven—are all the men who think they are taller than in fact they are. When I respond to the ad of a man who is the same 5'7" that I am, invariably, his brand of 5'7" is two inches shorter than mine, making me feel ungainly all over again. While I complain about all this, the reality is that even if the photos in merchandise catalogs were perfect and truth in advertising laws pertained to the words of personal ads, mail/male order would still be nonsensical because it is always necessary to see a thing up close to judge its quality.

So why do I continue to shop via the mail? Well, in the case of general merchandise, there's the fact that every once in a while I get lucky. And this success on the merchandise side of things makes me hopeful that the same will be true for finding a man. Besides, where else am I to look for a guy? In my heart I know that the best way to find a man is in pursuing my daily activities, but where do I go each day? To the market? To the cleaners? To my post-office box to see if my mail-order male has written back? Well, maybe . . .

Today I stopped by the post office for that exact purpose and William was there. I confessed to him the reason for my visit and was surprised by his response— instead of a lecture, he asked me out on a date. It seems that his wife has left him, which explains the fact that lately he's been commenting on my earrings, plucking stray hairs off my shoulders, and telling me that I look younger than my driver's license says. I chuckle over this turn of events and wonder if the winner in this male-order business could possibly be this U.S. Male.

Personal Ads:
A How-To

❦

I have heard it said that most books have at most two or three ideas to espouse and all the rest is explanation and example of those ideas, variations upon those themes. With that thought in mind, I have often wished—particularly when given a work of nonfiction—that I could just see the author's bare-bones outline and dispense with all those pages of amplification. I must admit that this was my initial feeling as I read *How to Find a Fella in the Want Ads,* by Zippy Larson. Three things fueled my need for brevity. First was Zippy's confession up front that the original manuscript had been "short and to the point, [not] even long enough to be a book." Second was the fact that I feared Zippy's homey writing would become cloying. And finally, I just wanted the scoop—how *do* you find a man in the want ads? By book's end, however, I had learned a lot, had been comforted by her philosophy, and was sorry to run out of words to read.

Zippy's method for working the personal ads was

contrary to my natural inclination. Jewish American Princess that I am, I have years of experience as a shopper and little experience in sales. So when I think of the personals, I think of shopping the ads, not running one. Additionally, whenever I have turned to the personals, I have done so in a desperate frame of mind, wanting a man and wanting him now. Placing an ad was never considered, therefore, because of the time required to get it in print. To all of this, Zippy would say, "Wrong, wrong, wrong." First of all, there's the time element. Patience is a virtue to Zippy, who states that her system will take consistent effort over a period of one to two years to be successful. Next, if a woman is really serious about finding a fella, then she must run the ad. And it isn't exactly one ad that we're talking about either; it's lots of ads, indeed, continuous ads, week after week and month after month until a prince is found. According to Zippy, the result of all of these ads is a large number of responses. Paradoxically, therefore, by becoming the salesperson and running the ads, we ultimately become the shopper, with a plethora of men from which to choose.

I have long felt that a woman could find a man if given a stack of them to sort through but have always wondered where she could find the stack. Zippy's system solves that problem.

A recurring topic in Zippy's book is the safety factor in meeting so many strangers. She continuously acknowledges that there are dangerous men in the world while giving specific methods for remaining safe when using the personals. For instance, she suggests using a post-office box for contact with the men so that a woman's address and phone number do not enter the picture. She also stresses meeting a man at a rendezvous point as opposed to ever getting into his car in the early days of the friendship. Making no apology for such caution, she suggests that a woman tell the man all the rules by which she needs to play in order to feel safe and to use his reaction as a gauge in judging him!

Another recurring concept in the book is the mindset needed in finding a man. Young folks may be put off by her comments while older ones will find them wise. She is not looking for love at first sight or even an instant spark, but instead tells us, "A person of fine character reveals himself in subtle ways, slowly. Kindness and a good heart aren't blaring like a TV commercial. Finding a gem takes looking and checking but mainly, patience." This doesn't mean that a spark isn't vital to a relationship; it's just a recognition that some fires are slow to start. Her very practical advice is, "if a man doesn't scare or offend you," go out with him a few times to see what develops.

So there in the barest of bones are the three main ideas in Zippy's book. The persistent placement of ads, along with the development of a danger detector, and the willingness to wait, will yield a marvelous mate. Does her system work? It did for Zippy and her husband, Lou—why not for you?

The Hug and Kiss Test

Put a penny in the *pishke!* Last Sunday I had not one but two dates. I can't figure out how it happened, as I am a woman whose phone no longer rings—even the telephone solicitors have ceased to show interest. Still, last week two men called to ask me out, one for morning coffee and the other for dinner, and I said yes to both.

I was doing three things I love when I happened to meet man number one—I was visiting a bookstore, drinking coffee in their café, and writing my column. The column dealt with the personal ads, so when this guy approached me and asked what I was writing, he learned quickly that I am a single female in search of a male, no sly winks on the side necessary. As for man number two, I answered his personal ad as I . . . uh . . . "researched" that topic for my column. I wrote him, he wrote back, and then we had two long telephone conversations, the second of which ended with his nebulous suggestion that we meet for coffee "sometime."

Two days later, he called again, got specific about Sunday, and upgraded me to dinner at the Olive Garden.

As I anticipated both dates, it was soothing to know what man number one looked like. He in fact looked quite nice, having thick, wavy hair that begged touching, sky blue eyes, and a grin—not smile—that let me know he was quite the *mazik*. He looked like a young Ted Koppel and had an equally wonderful vocabulary and voice. As for the sight-unseen man number two, I was worried. I remember seeing a greeting card with a gorgeous hunk of a man on the front and a *zhlub* of a man inside. The first picture was captioned, "What we're looking for," and the second, "What's looking for us." That was my fear exactly. Additionally, man number two was many years older than I, which was fine if he ended up looking like Robert Redford, but not so fine if a Woody Allen. So what did he look like? Well, like my cousin Kenny, who looks like actor Dick Van Patten, a real *haimisher* sort of guy.

I wasn't nervous about either date, as talking to men is no problem for me. I ask lots of questions and they feel flattered and answer. For those men who are into monosyllables, I use my experience as a motivational speaker to have a perfectly wonderful time talking out loud to myself. But as it turned out with both of these guys, the talking was an easy give and take. The Koppel-esque and I chatted away for two hours and the Van Pattenish and I for four. Indeed, Mr. Van Patten passed the all-important "time flies" test. We were shocked when our waitress told us that it was eleven o'clock and the restaurant was closing—four hours had passed as one.

After listening to the book-length version of this story, my girlfriends informed me that I liked these guys, particularly the time pilot. It sure looks like that on paper—and I didn't even mention that both of these men had truly fine relationships with their mothers, which wins lots of Brownie points in my book. But still, I don't know. I am normally the queen of hugs, hugging every man, woman, and child in my path, but as I left these guys and thought about hugging them goodbye, I quickly vetoed the idea. And when my daughter asked if either had kissed me, I cringed at the thought.

In spite of these failures at the hug and kiss test, I persist in considering second dates with these men. A "bird in the hand" mentality suggests itself to me as does the logical understanding that some relationships need time to grow. But as I say these things to myself, I laugh scornfully and shake my head in disgust, knowing that some element of flirtation, laughter, or joy must be evident in order to go back for more. Without these factors, I am making do and settling for far less than I want. The simple truth of the matter is that there are a lot of men in the world who are basically attractive and easy to talk to and who have many fine personality traits but with whom I do not wish to spend the rest of my life or even another hour on a Sunday.

A Recipe for Romance—and for Blintze Soufflé

It was summertime and I had a bad case of the blues. I was cranky and out of sorts and nothing pleased me. After quizzing me about my malaise, a friend suggested I do something fun and asked if I had any ideas. All I could think of was lounging before a roaring fire, though I knew I was a season or two away from that particular delight. My friend, however, saw no obstacle to my desire. Reminding me that my home had both central air-conditioning and a set of gas logs in the fireplace, she told me to crank both up to "high" and to have a good time. And that's exactly what I did.

In the years since that first summer fire, I have repeated the experience with some regularity. The emotional warmth of the fireplace does wonders for my soul and the oddity of the experience affords me a vacation from reality. Beyond that, since I am the quintessential good girl, it's a real kick to be so impractical, and perhaps even naughty, as to forget about the electric bill—and what my parents would think—and just have fun. All of these factors conspire to make a summer fire the perfect idea for a date with that special someone. I tried it, I liked it, and I recommend it heartily to others, sharing now all the ingredients for fireplace fun.

Since no Jewish event is complete without food, my afternoon before the fire becomes a picnic and the menu is my first consideration. Champagne or sparkling cider in tall goblets is a must and juicy summer fruits cut into finger-size pieces a nice accompaniment. The main dish, however, is debatable. Cheese and crackers are simple, filling, and easy to eat on the floor by the fire, but they lack a key element, aroma. I remember reading an article about selling residential real estate that suggested the slow roasting of dinner in the oven during an afternoon open house so as to snare a potential buyer through his sense of smell. I think the same lure will work with a lover. You just need the right recipe, and this is it—*blintze* soufflé. Start with a box of six frozen cheese blintzes. Place them in a casserole dish and pour half a stick of melted margarine or butter over them. Mix together three eggs, one tablespoon of vanilla, two tablespoons of orange juice, one cup of *smetteneh,* and three tablespoons of sugar. Beat these ingredients until frothy, pour them over the blintzes, and bake uncovered at 350 degrees for sixty to seventy-five minutes, until the soufflé is puffed and golden and the house smells heavenly. A little jam served on the side is nice . . . fun . . . exciting . . . and that same jam may be spread on toasted English muffins and topped with whipped cream. . . . I'll say no more.

If for our romantic tête-à-tête we can learn key ingredients from realtors, we can also learn from educators. Such professionals tell us that different people have different styles of learning. Some are visual learners, who need to take in words or images through their eyes. Others are auditory learners, who need to be told about the world. And still others are tactile learners, who need to write down what they see or hear or otherwise physically manipulate objects. A good teacher, therefore, will appeal to as many senses as possible to be effective, and this model holds true for creating the perfect date as well. To capture a man's attention, it is important to attack him through all of his senses.

This, then, is the recipe for summer romance. Start with the shocking visual image of a fire in the hearth. Place olfactory incentives in the very air he breathes. Mix in a variety of taste-bud treats. Add the sound of music in the form of Vivaldi's *Four Seasons,* the perfect accompaniment for winter-in-summer fun, and sprinkle tactile stimulation over all. Allow these ingredients to simmer for two to three hours until the relationship begins to thicken. A little flirtatious conversation served on the side is nice . . . fun . . . exciting . . . and should cause him to come back for more.

And there you have it, the perfect date with that special someone—an emotionally warm vacation from reality that is nicely naughty. Crank yourselves up to "high" and have a good time!

Have I Mentioned That I'm Jewish?

When it comes to dating, I am nonsectarian. I have gone out with men of many religions and far more non-Jews than Jews. This fact of my life is odd, particularly when I admit that, though I am not paranoid about anti-Semitism, I am certainly squeamish and ever cognizant of it, having experienced enough of it to know that it still exists. Therefore, when I meet a new man, I make a point of letting him know up front that I am a Jew, long before he has the opportunity to tell me about his latest purchase at the car dealership where he Jewed some salesman down a few hundred bucks. After I break the news to him, I hold my breath and pray for the resumption of normal conversation, pray that he won't ask me about some random Jew who lived in town twenty years ago to show that he once knew one.

My simultaneous interest in and worry about inter-religious dating stems from a childhood experience. I was born and raised in a St. Louis suburb called

University City. In the 1950s and early 1960s it was a predominantly Jewish community, which we lovingly nicknamed U. City and then Jew City. Living in that town, I never knew I was a minority. As the 1960s rolled along, however, the community opened itself up to other religions and races, and as the real world entered, I began to learn that I was "different." My education in this regard came when I was a teenager babysitting for a non-Jewish woman who was thirty years old, educated, intelligent, and shocked to learn from meeting me that Jews do not have horns. (I am not kidding.) It hurt my feelings that she thought such a thing, and from that moment forth, I became a "Jewish evangelist," spreading the word—by my very presence—that Jews are human.

As an adult I have struggled over the issue of interreligious dating and marriage. On the one hand, I want Jews to remain separate so as not to complete Hitler's work through assimilation, but on the other hand, I want the various faiths to mix it up in order to put an end to prejudice based on theology. I do not think it was God's plan for religion to separate people. I do not think He intended for there to be holy wars on the grand scale or prejudicial words like "kike"—or perhaps even "*shaygetz*" and "*shiksa*"—on the small scale. Being that evangelist again, I think what He intended is love.

Resolving this issue on a personal level, I married a Jewish man in my twenties and produced three Jewish children. Now I date whomever I please, looking more to spirituality than religion. I don't care what road a man takes to get to God—or godliness—just as long as he gets there.

All of this brings me to Jake, a Catholic man I once dated. Mall walkers both, we met while doing our laps. Within minutes I told him a JAP joke to fill him in on my Jewishness. He laughed at the joke and took the news in his stride as we talked easily, laughed a lot, and marveled over the many things we had in common. Months into our friendship, he pointed out another mall walker to me. "See that woman?" he asked. "I used to look at her and think, 'I bet she's Jewish.'" I was looking at a blond, fair-skinned woman and did not agree, but let him continue, a little shocked to hear that he spent his time picking Jews out of the crowd. "Turns out that she sings in the choir at my church." After laughing over his story, I suggested to Jake that I came into his life to teach him a thing or two about Jews—including tolerance—and he didn't argue. He just took it in his stride.

That same day, Jake and I passed a mirror at the mall and stopped to have a look. There he stood in his fair-haired and pink-skinned glory as I stood dark haired and olive skinned in mine, and we were amazed, amazed that we could be so very different while being so much alike. This, of course, is my point exactly and the reason why I am nonsectarian in my dating. I choose to date men, not religions, looking for what I think is God's plan—love.

Regarding Corn, Nuns, and Strawberries

Last Friday was an extraordinary day. I spent it as a volunteer worker at an organic farm in southeast Indiana. Michaela Farm is owned by the Sisters of St. Francis and it coexists with the mother house on 350 acres. My friend Jet is the head of personnel at the farm and it was his birthday. His simple request for a gift was that I spend the day and so I did.

Because he thinks me quite the baleboosteh, Jet's first assignment for me was in the kitchen. Lunch was going to be *yontifdik* that day as we celebrated his birthday, and so I helped (Sister) Anita prepare a large meal. One of my tasks was to shuck corn. Of course, I had shucked grocery-store corn in the past, so I knew that not every cob is perfect. But I somehow expected perfection from this corn that was right off the stalk and was surprised to find that only one in four cobs looked like the ones that Green Giant sells in my grocer's freezer case. It made me wonder if this corn had self-esteem issues, as did I. Did it compare itself to the Green Giant variety? Did it consider a "beauty makeover," with some kernels getting "highlighted" to bring them up to yellow perfection and others getting "implants" to make them *zaftik?* Or did it know that being odd and imperfect was normal, and did it appreciate the fact that it was nutritious and delicious to boot?

When it was time to eat that corn and all the other products of Anita's and my labor, fourteen of us gathered for a communal *brokheh.* Standing and holding hands around the long farm table, we each mentioned something for which we were grateful that day, and then we heaped our plates and ate. Between mouthfuls of food, we shared stories of our lives according to a tradition at the farm—each person told a story about what was happening in their life when they were the age of the birthday person. Since Jet was fifty-three and one of the elder statesmen at the farm, participants could choose to tell stories of their lives at thirty-five, five, three, or even eight!

I was touched by the stories I heard that day, as many were quite revealing, but the one that affected me most was told by Sister Claire. When she was fifty-three years old she had to change her living situation because of a relationship conflict with another nun. Her story surprised me, sounding so similar to my own divorce and then subsequent movement into and out of a love relationship with another man. Of course, I have a lot of experience with people and so I know that not every relationship can be perfect. But from a nun, an emissary of God, I somehow expected perfection and was surprised to learn that interpersonal relationships can be difficult for all of us who are mortal.

Though we lingered over lunch, storytelling, carrot cake, apple cobbler, and ice cream, we eventually made it back into the fields to work. My afternoon assignment was to be a part of the "strawberry liberation front." Quite simply, on an organic farm, weed killers are not used, and it was our task to free the strawberry patch from the many weeds that threatened to choke it. I loved pulling the weeds, loved knowing that my efforts would literally bear fruit, loved imagining that the same could hold true in my life if I were to identify and pull some weeds there too.

My day at the farm was extraordinary and what made it so was mindfulness. Usually I rush from task to task in my life and glory only in the fact that I can cross one off my list. At the farm, each action offered more. I unsheathed corn and truths. I listened to others and learned. I pulled weeds and pondered. It was a wonderful day, and thus my last act as a farmer was to stop at the farm's Contemplation House to give thanks. Sitting on a meditation cushion with a wonderful breeze blowing in, I forgave myself for the ways in which I am not perfect and thanked God for a day that was.

On the Fritz

My mother is not a man. This simple truth has major repercussions. Namely, when she gives me advice on home repair, I don't take her seriously. Instead I scoff and think, "What does she know?" I recently gave her the lowdown on my DustBuster®, telling her it sounded funny, was somehow anemic, and could no longer suck things up. She told me that DustBusters only cost thirty dollars and suggested I buy a new one. That's not what I wanted to hear! I wanted her to tell me how to *patshke* with it for five minutes as my ex-husband would have and make it work again.

Since she's absolutely useless to me in these situations, I didn't bother to tell her about the *tsores* I was having with my garage-door opener. The remote-control unit had ceased to function reliably. It often worked when I had to lower the door as I was leaving but rarely worked when I had to raise it again upon returning home. I tried a new battery to no avail, and then I called a repairman, with "man" being the operative word.

My home has a two-car garage, but instead of having one big garage door, it has two smaller ones and thus twice as many things that can go wrong. Therefore, Rob, the garage-door guy, has visited my home frequently through the years. What I like about him is that he knows his stuff. He can virtually disassemble and reassemble a garage-door opener without looking. He stands upon his little stepstool pedestal, arms overhead, battery-powered screwdriver whirring, as he gives me eye contact and kibitzes away.

Rob paid me a visit on Monday. Well, to be more precise, I paid Rob to visit me on Monday. After I explained the problem to him, he took the remote-control unit and pushed the button. Luckily for me, it was still broken—the little red light came on to show that the battery was working, but the door did not go up. Rob got a testing device from his truck and pushed the button again. The signal emitted by my hand unit was thus converted into a musical tone and Rob didn't like what he heard. He got a new garage-door clicker from his truck and let it sing into the device, at which time we heard an entirely different sound. Rob's diagnosis was that my garage opener sounded funny, was somehow anemic, and could no longer lift garage doors up. His prescription was that I buy a new one. Surprise, surprise, they cost thirty dollars.

As part of the house call, Rob proceeded to do routine maintenance on my garage doors. With a bzzz, bzzz, bzzz of his power tool he tightened bolts on the hinges, and with a psst, psst, psst he sprayed lubricant here and there. He suggested that I follow his lead and service the doors in this manner every few months.

Internally, a petulant voice scoffed at the notion, saying, "Well, OK, you teach me how to oil my springs and I'll teach you how season a fry pan. What, are you crazy?!" Externally, I just smiled pleasantly and nodded.

When his work was done, Rob presented me with his bill—$109, broken down as follows: a $39 trip charge, $40 for a half-hour of labor, and $30 for the new clicker. Strangely, he charged me nothing for the lessons of the day, which can be itemized in this manner: home repair is not something that only men know about, I could learn to psst and bzzz if I were so inclined, and my ambivalence and fussiness over doing so stem from a deep-seated desire to keep traditional male and female roles separate and to have some man perform his assigned tasks in return for me performing mine.

Before leaving, Rob asked if there was anything else I needed him to do. My mind immediately went to the crack in the basement wall that needed sealing, the desk drawer that only opened halfway, and, of course, the new DustBuster that needed to be mounted on the wall, but I didn't think that was what he had in mind. Besides, he was already down off his pedestal, and so I just smiled pleasantly and said no.

What next? Well, I guess I'll call Mom for some advice, as she really seems to know her stuff . . . even though she's not a man.

Beer Halls and Pizza Parlors

We all play many roles in life, some comfortable, some not. It was odd for me last Wednesday, therefore, to play parts from the disparate ends of the comfort spectrum both in the same night. But play them I did, being first a mommy person on an outing to a pizza parlor and then a swinging single at a bar.

One of my oldest and favorite roles is that of mother, but I don't get to play it very frequently these days as two of my three children are grown and my "little one" is a teenager, with very little time for her mom. Luckily for me, Lisa's best friend is away for many weeks this summer and in her absence I have become my daughter's playmate. Seeking fun things for us to do, I happened upon a coupon for Chuck E. Cheese Pizza Parlor—a large pizza, soft drinks, and ninety (ninety!) game tokens all for $27.99. *Takheh a metsieh* to be sure, but also a perfect activity for us. Though seventeen years old, Lisa still likes to play arcade games that pay off in tickets that she can later trade in for a prize. She gets this propensity from me, a woman who orders Happy Meals™ at McDonald's for the sake of the toy.

If "eat, drink, and be merry" is a goal in life, we accomplished it in our three hours at the pizza parlor, getting absolutely *ongeshtopt* on pizza and unlimited pop and acting our shoe size instead of our age with the games. Though we won many tickets at the basketball toss and Skee-Ball, our favorite game by far was one in which we inserted our token and watched it drop onto a platform with hundreds of other tokens, which then got pushed toward a ledge by three little rakes. Tickets spewed forth from the machine whenever one of the coins fell off the ledge, and bunches of them were always half a smidge away from taking the plunge. One of the biggest challenges in playing the game was this (other) little girl who always wanted a turn. Sometimes we gave it to her and other times we giggled madly and continued to play until eventually we ran out of tokens. Rich in tickets at that point, we headed to the emporium, where we traded all 335 of them in on a figurine, two plastic bracelets, and a bag of cotton candy. Eight nights of Chanukah presents couldn't have tickled us more.

It was after nine o'clock when we got home, which is usually time for me to *mach nacht,* but that was not the case on Wednesday. Instead, I had plans with Mary, a friend who has taken it upon herself to make me less of a homebody and fuddy-duddy. Never married and forty-three, she is to me the epitome of a single woman. She has a high-powered job and all the independence that goes with it; she is blond, beautiful, and built and has more male admirers than I have Happy Meal toys; and she knows everything happening in our city. Our evening's plan was to meet downtown at the BarrelHouse Brewing Company to hear the band in which her brother plays. There was no way I could say no to going, but really, me in a bar? I don't even drink . . . except when I'm with Mary.

The BarrelHouse was intimidating to me in many ways. First, I had to go downtown at night and face bad neighborhoods, one-way streets, and limited parking. Then, I had to worry about bar basics—where do you order, when do you pay, what kind of tip is customary, and do people really order rounds for their whole party or is that just on TV? And if that wasn't enough, I also had to approach Mary's table of male and female friends and hope for a turn to "play." But somehow I managed to do it all—and have a great time in the process.

As I reviewed the experience on my way home, the child in me clamored for a prize for making it through the night. So I gave myself the Academy Award for the best performance by a childlike actress in an adult role. I even gave an acceptance speech. "Aw, shucks," I said, "anyone can stretch and play a new role, so I encourage you to try it too. Eat, drink, and be Mary!"

Feelings for a Man

It's been a week now that his house has been dark, not to mention the fact that last week at this time his trashcans were pulled to the curb a full two days in advance of pickup. I try to believe that he and his wife and children are off on vacation somewhere . . . Disney World would be nice . . . but I know that I am the one in Fantasy Land. The darkened house is a product of divorce and he has moved away.

It was several months ago that my friend Bea mentioned him to me over lunch. She was surprised that I didn't know him, as she thought he lived very close to my house. She told me that he was a wonderful man, a professional, and Jewish to boot and that he was either divorced or soon to be. Though she did not offer to play *shadchen,* she suggested I get to know him. Uncertain as to how I might pull off such a stunt, I gave him no further thought.

Within a couple weeks of the conversation, however, I happened to see his name on a donor list from our local high school. That very same day, I saw his wife's name and photograph in our Jewish newspaper. Being one who takes a coincidence as a meant-to-be, I felt compelled to find out more about him. So I looked him up in the phone book, where I learned that his street was one I passed every morning on my walk. On the next day's stroll I realized that I not only knew his house—the one that was always lit up—but I also "knew" him, as he was the well-dressed, predawn dog walker whom I passed daily. I had never said hello to him because he was always so lost in a sad reverie. Now I knew why. If in my wildest dreams I had hoped to feel something for Bea's friend one day, the raw pain of his divorce was not what I had in mind. But that's exactly what seeing him and knowing about him engendered in me for weeks to come.

As a veteran of divorce, I know that the experience is quite *geferlekh*. Even in the worst of marriages, it is wrenching to leave. I have a friend, for instance, whose husband beat her and threatened her life for more than a quarter-century and even for her, divorce was not a joyous moment, just a necessary action. Even in less dramatic cases, the same is often true. What is also true, however, is that, as hard as it is to leave an unhappy marriage, it can be equally hard to stay.

Life inside an emotionally dead marriage was depicted in a scene from *The Good Mother,* a book by Sue Miller. In it, a woman tells her adult granddaughter, "There was a period in my life where I used to wake up each morning and wish I'd died. Just wished I'd passed away in the night. I never would have done anything, you know, but each day I'd open my eyes sorry that I had to." This period lasted for ten or fifteen years (!!) and ended when love reentered her life in the form of a change-of-life baby. I found the scene to be a chilling and graphic description of such a marriage. It made me realize that difficult as divorce is, it is certainly better than a life spent wishing for death.

It was with all these thoughts tearing at my heart that I witnessed the last gasp of Bea's friend's marriage when I saw the For Sale and Sold signs go up on his house all on the same day. The Sold sign stayed up for little more than a week, giving the realtor his due while sparing the man unnecessary pain. And then as quickly as the signs had come and gone, the lights went out in the house, filling me with pain. I had hoped for a miracle for this man and his family, but apparently none was forthcoming. Instead of a change-of-life baby, they got life changes.

I continue to feel for the man, wherever he may be, and I wish him well. May each step he takes with his little doggie carry him farther from the pain of divorce, and may love in some form soon reenter his life, filling his heart and new home with light.

Long Sleeves in Summer

Every Tuesday my local newspaper publishes a list of the "Tristate's Most Wanted." The mug shots of ten criminals are shown and I find myself scanning the page for men I have dated. It's not that I date men of questionable character; it's just that when I am dating complete strangers, I never really know. Some of the guys on the list look wild-eyed and crazy, but others look, if not like the man next door, then certainly like the one I chatted with as I waited for a plane at the airport. I laugh at myself for perusing the list and congratulate myself too. It is wise to be wary.

Back in the old days, dating safety was not an issue. The boys I dated in high school were the same ones I attended birthday parties for in kindergarten. I knew those guys through and through. I knew their parents and pets, their synagogues and scout troops, their reputations as students and sportsmen and sons. I was safe in their cars and safe in their homes. I remember the oddity, therefore, of going to college and meeting new guys about whom I knew nothing. I was consciously aware of the safety net lacking as I tried dating them and was not at all comfortable. My fear was enhanced on a date during freshman year. It was a fall day and the young man and I were out for a walk. We passed a card shop with *shanah-tovas* displayed in the window. This was his lead-in to announcing that he didn't like Jews, that in fact, none of his family did. Trust me, I chose to flee without waiting to find out what their solution might be to the "problem" of the Jew.

As intimidating as dating was in college, at least I knew that any guy I met there had a background similar to mine—he valued education and performed well enough in life to be accepted to a school. But now that I am a midlife dater, even this layer of safety falls away, for when I meet a man out and about, or when I answer a personal ad, I know no such thing about him. I try to pick the ones who "look" safe, but I know that even a *vilde mensch* could masquerade in Prince Charming's clothing.

I realize, therefore, that if I don't want to get *geharget*, it pays to remember a few rules for dating safely. I know that I should not immediately give out my full name, address, and phone number. I know that I should not allow him to pick me up at my home but that we should meet at a public and nonsecluded place. I know that if we move on from the original date site to a new one, I should travel there in my own car. And I know that no matter how nice a time we have, I should not invite him back to my place nor go to his until I know him better. I also know that I should give a friend all the specifics of the date, the who, what, when, and where, so that in the worst-case scenario, the cavalry can come to my rescue.

While all of these safety tips are valuable, the most important is this—I need to trust my instincts. This, then, brings me to Art, a man I met at an ice-cream parlor. He was handsome, easy to talk to, and obviously very intelligent. But he also had a spotty work history in an industry that I did not respect, his clothes were slightly *shlumperdik*, and, oddly, he had on a heavy long-sleeve shirt in the middle of summer. Something about him didn't add up, but, giving him the benefit of the doubt, I agreed to see him again a week later. When I did, he still wore long sleeves. Of course, there's probably a logical explanation—he gets cold in air-conditioning or has a scar or tattoo he tries to hide—but that's not where my mind went. I was thinking track marks.

Maybe I'm wrong. Maybe he's not wanted for possession of dangerous drugs. Maybe he's wanted for aggravated murder instead, or maybe he's a truly great guy. But my instincts tell me that something's not kosher and so I listen, because when dating a complete stranger, it is *always* wise to be wary.

The A's Marry the B's

Dr. Daugherty was my English literature professor in college. While I have forgotten everything he taught me about *The Canterbury Tales* and *Sir Gawain and the Green Knight*, I do remember two things from his class. First, though I don't recall what a lyric poem is, I remember that he said all such poems had the same message—"I hurt." Second, I remember that on the last day of class he interrupted the final exam to read us a poem he had just written about two lovers he spotted from our classroom window. In it he made the observation that in college classrooms where students are seated alphabetically, the A's marry the B's. I have finally figured out a practical application for these bits of information and here it is—for all singles who "hurt" as they find their independent lives transmogrifying into loneliness, try joining a new group and, seated alphabetically or not, chat up the person sitting beside you.

I know that this is hardly a new idea, but an experience I had last week tells me it's a good one. My youngest child is beginning her senior year of high school and I attended a meeting for the parents of her class. I hate meetings, because I know that if there are thirty people present, they will have forty ideas to espouse and I get sick of listening, not to mention the fact that I've got work to do at home. But in spite of the fact that we hashed and rehashed the "how-to's" of getting all senior parents to chip in gelt for the year's events, the meeting was a delight because of the sense of community I felt there. I have known and worked with these other parents for all the years of my daughter's education, and I enjoyed shmoozing with them before and after the meeting—so much so, in fact, that I was the last person to leave. To borrow from the "Cheers" theme song, I loved being in a place where everybody knew my name.

Obviously, this parents' group was not chosen for its potential to bring eligible men into my life, but what if I were to join a group with that goal in mind? What if I gave time instead of money to my temple or to a charitable organization? Could it pay off in dates as opposed to tax deductions? Or what if I joined a professional organization in my field? Could it bring me a "leading man" instead of just leads? It certainly seems possible if I choose the group judiciously.

So what should I look for in a group? First, it must be coed, so I'll scratch the local quilt guild and women's networking group from consideration. Next, it must have a long history and still be going strong, so that it will continue to attract new members and still be in existence in five years when I finally get to know everyone. It should also offer lots of activities and subcommittees, so that I can find a project to work on that will be a good match for my interests and skills. The goal here is not just to belong to the group but also be involved. In this manner, people will come to see more of me than just my pretty face, or lack thereof. And as I choose the exact work to do for the group, I need to keep my goal in mind at all times. Thus, if I want to meet men of my own socioeconomic level and age, I should not do volunteer work in a soup kitchen or nursing home but instead serve those organizations by sitting on their boards.

Playing the devil's advocate, what if Dr. Daugherty was wrong about proximity promoting passion? What if group membership does not bring love my way? Well, I will still have done worthwhile work. I will still have filled otherwise boring evenings and weekends with places to go and people to see I will still have made dozens of new friends who will do more good for my life—in sickness and in health—than an equal number of pills or vitamin tablets. All of these factors will keep the positive aspects of aloneness from deteriorating into the hurt of loneliness. And instead of a lyric poem, my life will be a song—cheers!

Warning: X-Rated

I read a newspaper article recently about new words and expressions graduating from the vernacular and making it into the dictionaries of America. In it, AP writer Richard Pyle mentioned that *dot-com* got added to the lexicon this year, as did *24-7* and *energy bar*. He also gave an interesting six-decade retrospective of new terms. If I may share a lighthearted word per decade: we added *baby-sit, car wash, disco, junk food, channel surf,* and *bad hair day* as we progressed from the forties through the nineties. On a more serious note, we also added *atom bomb, aerospace, biohazard, sexism, AIDS,* and *World Wide Web* in the same time frame. After reading the article I was hungry for a follow-up piece, as I wondered what words have fallen from common usage, becoming archaic and obsolete. In particular, I wondered about one word—*promiscuous.*

Why does this word jump into my mind? It's because of a TV show I watched recently, a sitcom on HBO, "Sex and the City." It's a big hit. Sarah Jessica Parker is the lead actress in the series, playing the part of Carrie Bradshaw, a sex columnist and "sexual anthropologist" for the *New York Star.* To quote the show's Web site, "late-night cavorting and the sex lives of herself and her single friends are the fodder for Carrie's provocative writing on dating and mating in the concrete jungle." I have seen exactly one episode of the show and, quite frankly, I was appalled. Within the space of thirty minutes I was shown not one, not two, but three sexually explicit scenes involving Carrie's friend Samantha and a man referred to as her "pick of the week."

I could write many different columns on my response to this show. As a mother, I pull my hair over the fact that such sights are piped into the homes of America for our children to see. As a health fanatic, I scream over the complete disregard for safe sex inherent in such representations. But I confess that what I most objected to in the show was not the sex acts demonstrated, nor the fact that someone bothered to film such scenes and show them as entertainment, but the casual nature of the relationship in which the sex took place.

My dictionary defines *promiscuity* as engaging in sex indiscriminately or with many persons. This definition is subjective, leaving me to wonder what constitutes "indiscriminate" behavior, and what quantity of sex partners equals "many." In Samantha's case, a new man each week equals 52 lovers a year and 520 in a decade of "dating." Going out on a limb here, I'd call that promiscuous, though HBO would probably disagree as they hold her life up to viewers as an acceptable norm. Giving Samantha the benefit of the doubt, what if she only used the "pick of the month" system instead? That puts her down to 12 men a year and 120 in a decade. That's better. But is it good? And where do we draw the line? Should we only count on one set of fingers our lifetime lovers or can we use two? Is it all right for toes to enter the count?

There are no easy answers here. I am fully cognizant of the fact that it is a great challenge to juggle the polarities of being sexual but single adults, so I urge singles to actively think about their stand on this issue. My own position is this—as much as I yearn for warm arms to hold me, I want to find such arms within a meaningful relationship. This is because I believe that sex is a precious gift to be given and received, something akin to a twenty-dollar gold piece in mint condition as opposed to a crumpled dollar bill passed to and used by many.

If indeed the concept of promiscuity has fallen from circulation, I vote for its reinstatement. I also vote to add a few other words that give the message that a person can engage in too much casual sexual activity. Thus I nominate these Yiddish terms for inclusion in Webster's—*tsatske, hultie,* and *nafkeh.*

Sex is great. Sex with a conscience is better.

Amortization Charts

My friend Estee has been divorced for a year and she's desperately lonely. I give her my basic pep talk on the subject, telling her that life-expectancy charts prove that women live longer than men and all of us gals are bound to be alone in the end anyway. "Isn't it nice," I ask, "that we'll be so practiced in handling it?" She literally groans and tells me I'm being grim, so I try another tack. I explain mortgage amortization charts to her. "OK, Estee," I say, "here's how an amortization chart works. The monthly payment always remains the same but the amount going toward principal and interest changes every single month. In the first month, almost the entire payment goes toward interest, while only twenty or thirty dollars pays down the principal. After years and years and years, the principal and interest begin to get paid off equally, and by the end of the mortgage, almost all monies go toward the principal. Loneliness and the ability to have a full and happy life are the interest and principal of single-hood, and with every passing month the loneliness subsides." Having a year's firsthand experience with a home mortgage and realizing that she really does feel less lonely and pained now than she did on day one of her divorce, Estee falls for my words.

I must admit that most of the time I fall for them too, but there are times when no amount of coaxing or logical thinking on the topic impresses me and I feel lonely—all right, desperately lonely—too. When in such a mood I often choose to get lost in a book, and that's how I came to read two novels by Jane Shapiro. *The Dangerous Husband* called to me from my library's new-release shelf. It's a small book, a black comedy, dealing with the demise of a marriage. Its rendering of male-female relationships was so astute and funny that on several occasions I laughed until I cried and then I cried until I wheezed. Wanting to read more of Shapiro's work, I found her first book, *After Moondog*. This one had all the tears without the laughter as she wrote about topics too close to home. Part one dealt with the demise of a woman's marriage, part two with her harrowing experiences in raising two teenagers alone, and part three with her total involvement in her elderly mother's widowhood and subsequent cancer diagnosis.

Though the book touched me on many levels, my strongest reaction to *After Moondog* was anger with the elderly mother for her constant kvetching about being alone and her endless quest to find a man. I realize fully that I identified with the woman and was really angry with myself, but at any rate, I wanted to shake her and tell her there's more to life than men. It reminded me of a story about my bubbie. As a gift for her ninety-somethingth birthday, her children gave her a dress that she tried on and immediately insisted they return, saying it made her look fat. I nearly plotzed! Even in old age we women are going to worry about our weight? Even in old age we're going to moan about men? *Genug iz genug.* Let's just get on with life!

Comparing Shapiro's two books may hold the key to doing just that. *The Dangerous Husband* was a compact tale with a definite beginning, middle, and end—girl meets boy, girl marries boy, relationship turns dangerously sour and must end. Complete closure was achieved with the death of one of the spouses. *After Moondog* was nothing at all like that. Instead it was a continuing saga of life flowing from pain to pain and then through several occasions of joy before going back to pain again. As I came to the end of part one and ached with the character's grief, I wondered how on earth "we" would resolve such anguish. I anxiously turned the page to see, only to find that the next chapter took place several years later. I was angry with the author for writing in this manner. "Come on, Jane Shapiro," I shouted, "tell me how to make such pain subside!" When I calmed down, however, I realized that she had done just that. Pain is like an amortization chart. After years and years and years it does subside. Passage of time is the answer. Just get on with life!

The Scent of a Man

My friend Roberta was in a relationship with a man for more than a decade. The relationship was unfulfilling and going no place but still she remained within it. It is now a handful of years later, and all she can say to explain the attraction is that she thinks it had something to do with his scent. Though I personally would follow a man to the ends of the earth if he wore patchouli oil or Tsar cologne, that's not what Roberta had in mind. She was talking about a natural scent, perhaps one that is only noticed subliminally.

I had trouble understanding Roberta's point until I met a man named Kerry. Though we had a lot in common and our first date was an exciting talkfest, I doubted that we would be anything more than friends because he was too old for me. More than that, there was this oddity—he physically resembled my grandpa, making it seem incestuous for us ever to be romantically linked. Let me note that it is my habit to hug people as I say hello and goodbye, and thus I hugged Kerry twice on our first date. After he left I giggled on the phone with girlfriends about the incongruity and impossibility of dating a grandpa lookalike. Once off the phone, however, I noticed something strange. His scent was on my body from our hugs. No, I don't mean his cologne—he wasn't wearing any—and no, I don't mean a soap-and-water smell or its opposite, Eau de Shvitz. I don't fully understand what it was. All I can say is that I could smell him even though he was gone. His scent was intoxicating and irresistible, making me like a cartoon character struck over the head and seeing stars. The dialog balloon read, *"Boing!"* And I was hooked.

Modern science offers a possible explanation of this experience in its study of pheromones. A pheromone is described as an odor produced by an animal that affects the behavior of other animals. It is thought to be the most ancient form of animal communication, and since the 1980s scientists have believed it may function in humans as well. Whereas the human sense of smell operates on a conscious level, human pheromones work in astonishingly small concentrations below what the sense of smell can detect. In other words, pheromones perform on the unconscious level. The translation of this is that if human pheromones are indeed at work, we may not even know what has hit us—boing!

Another possible explanation for Roberta's and my experiences would be in keeping with Pavlov and his dog. As you may recall, whenever the dog was given food, a bell was sounded, until the dog came to salivate not only at the sight of food but also at the sound of the bell, even if no food was presented. Extrapolating from

Pavlov's dog, perhaps all people have a subliminal scent and we have olfactory memories of people we have known and loved in the past. When we see that old love again, or even smell someone with a similar scent, good feelings wash over us as we subconsciously go on a scent-imental journey.

Whether either of these explanations pertains is anyone's guess, but the importance of the sense of smell in the selection of a partner is interesting to consider. No one questions the idea that we are attracted to some men because of the way they look. Nor is it ludicrous to believe that we may be drawn to a guy because of his deep, rich, or mellifluous voice. It only seems logical, therefore, that the scent of a man is part of the package that interests us. What is the implication of this for dating singles? We need to get close enough to a man to allow the *schnoz* to be part of the selection process. Sit next to him instead of across from him at a restaurant. Consider a night of dancing in his arms. Lean into him at the symphony or theater and whisper a thing or two in his ear. Remember to hug him as you say hello and goodbye. And in each and every one of these cases, remember to inhale him. In this manner, you will find out exactly what it is that the nose knows and, surprisingly, it may be a lot. Ladies, clear your nasal passages. Let the sniffing begin!

She's One of Those

In her adult life, my friend Lois has been a beauty-pageant queen, furrier's model, and charm-school teacher. She is chic, sophisticated, and a hard act to follow. We recently spent a weekend together at her time-share condominium in Myrtle Beach. At the pool she wore a sexy black swimsuit from the Victoria's Secret catalog, while I wore a T-shirt and shorts. I try not to hold this against her.

Lois and I go back to 1981 as neighbors and book-club friends. During our years together, we have witnessed great changes in each other's lives, as she became a widow and I a divorcee. This has given us an additional bond as we now have our lives as swinging singles to compare. Thus, as we sat around the pool, Lois told me about the two men she was dating. One was a prominent man a few years older than she, who squired her to fine restaurants and the theater in his BMW. The other was a fun-loving man fifteen years her junior who took her to rodeos in his vintage red

Corvette convertible. She said that in the course of a weekend she often went from pearls and high heels to jeans and cowboy boots, and she was having a grand time in the process. I, on the other hand, was not dating anyone at the time. But of course, I didn't hold that against her either.

To drive home the point of what a truly amazing character my friend Lois is, I should mention another of our disparities—our ages. Lois just had a seventieth birthday, while I am forty-eight. From the start, the age difference was one of the things that pulled us together. Lois, being more than just a pretty face, is a strong woman who has endured many personal tragedies. When we first met, she had just lost her youngest daughter in a car accident. In a heartbreaking twist of fate, Denise was buried on what would have been her twenty-second birthday. In another twist of fate, I entered Lois's life a year later, resembling Denise. While neither of us was looking for a mother/daughter relationship, this certainly set us up for a unique friendship.

In bits and snatches over the years, I had heard the story of Denise, but while in Myrtle Beach, Lois put all the pieces together. She told of the days and weeks in which she cried continuously from ten o'clock until two. She told of a friend's eventual urging that she try to get out of the house. She told of her decision, therefore, to play racquetball, with the thought of taking her bitterness out on the ball. And she also told of a call she received on the day she got the courage to do just that. It was from a member of a support group for people who had suffered loss. This other woman couldn't believe Lois would choose to play a sport rather than come to a meeting and said that Lois was "one of those" who would have a nervous breakdown in the future because of her denial.

Lois was far too gracious to argue with the woman, so she made her rebuttal to me. She said everyone must go through grief but each person walks through it at his or her own speed. Surprisingly, however, there does come a day when that person can go to the grocery store, hear the checker ask a friendly, "How are you today?" and not feel compelled to tell her but instead just say, "OK."

This hard-won knowledge helped Lois when she became a widow in 1991. As part of her walk through that grief, she moved to a new house. Interestingly, she did not downsize her home, because she felt that a small house implied a small life and she did not intend that for herself. Thus she has plenty of room to entertain her cocktail club, various bridge clubs, and book club. And she keeps busy with various sports including curling (!) and with work as a docent at a local historical site.

It used to be said of Timex watches that they take a licking and keep on ticking. The same may be said of Lois. Yes, she's "one of those," and I love her for it, even if she does look great in a sexy black swimsuit from Victoria's Secret.

An Interesting Man

I always keep an eye out for interesting men, and recently I found one! It was in the course of my early-morning walk. My current regimen takes me around two residential subdivisions and one strip shopping center, and this guy makes daily appearances at the outdoor mall. He's tall enough for me, about the right age (fifty-ish), and quite distinguished looking with a deep tan, thick head of gray hair, and well-trimmed mustache and beard. He looks like the kind of guy I could proudly take home to mother and who would fit in with my chic friends, my intellectual friends, and even my kids.

Every time I see this man I want to shout, "Hey good-lookin', care to join me on my walk?" Two things keep me from doing so. First is the fact that I would never say such a thing to a strange man, but beyond that, there is one odd detail about him that I failed to mention. What brings him to the mall each day is his job—he's the person who sweeps the parking lot. Since he looks like a man who could be the CEO of a major American corporation, I am rendered speechless. *Vos iz dos?* If I understand nothing else, at least I know where he gets his tan.

Trying to make sense of this incongruous picture, I fantasize various lives for the attractive sweeper. The worst-case scenario finds him as some sort of addict who between binges manages to get jobs involving menial labor. I tend to rule this possibility out because he is far too robust to be frequently wasted. Additionally, he seems so responsible, appearing every morning like clockwork.

Another imagined life is that after thirty years in corporate America he was offered and accepted a lucrative early-retirement package. Not one to sit home all day and tinker, he decided to get a stress-free job. After a stint as a greeter at Wal-Mart, he recognized his need to be outdoors and away from harried people. Dustpan and broom in hand, he is now working happily ever after on the parking lot of the outdoor mall.

A similar scenario has him walking away from his former profession but with no cushy retirement package in place. He remembered Lily Tomlin's joke, which says that the trouble with being in the rat race is even if you win, you are still a rat, and he decided to give up his rathood. Pursuing simplicity instead of affluence, he now works only enough to put a roof over his head and food on his table. Zen-like in his efforts, he is mindful as he sweeps trash and carries litter, and he is serene.

The final fantasy finds him as the owner of this and other strip malls. Tired of the pressures of running such vast real-estate holdings, he has turned the management of his properties over to a bunch of guys in suits while he keeps an eye on things from afar—the parking lot. He used to sweep at all of his properties, rotating them day by day, but since noticing me, he comes daily to my neighborhood to keep an eye on me as well.

And indeed, we seem to have each other in the cross hairs of our consciousness. He could be at the far corner of the parking lot when I first enter the area, but as soon as he spots me, he reins himself in, and by the time I walk to the end of the strip of stores, turn around, and come back, he is always within speaking distance. To speak or not to speak: that, then, is the question. Whether 'tis better to keep projecting lives upon him or to find out who he really is, is what I must decide. Though my cultural conditioning tells me that he could be a *meshuggener, shlemiel,* or *shlimazel,* my eyes tell me that he could easily be so much more. Which is the dream and which the reality? And do I have the courage to find out? To speak is perchance to shatter the dream. To speak is also the opportunity to enter it as I give the attractive sweeper his own voice, invite him to tell his own story, and see if it sweeps me off my feet. Hmmm . . . how tidy—perhaps I'll give it a try. How hard can it be to say, "Good morning"?

Perspective

After a twenty-seven-year hiatus, I am back in school. I find the experience to be humbling. I'm working toward certification in communication design, which means that I am learning about computer graphics, layout, typography, and the like. Since my 1973 bachelor's degree is not in fine arts, two basic drawing classes are required. I'm taking the first one now and a computer art class to boot. Both classes are difficult, frustrating, and stressful, bringing out all the Yiddish in me. I stand at my easel or sit at my computer and produce images at which I silently shriek, *"Got in himmel"* and *"Feh!"*

I was warned during Art Start, the new-student orientation session, that the program was very challenging. One of the professors said that at the three-week mark, most students are ready to run screaming from campus and forget about certification. Having now reached that point, I understand what she was talking about. What keeps me from quitting, however, is my own week-number-three phenomenon, which is that I noticed something interesting about my drawing teacher. He is a man. This startling realization occurred in the middle of class. He was pointing to another student's sketch, when mit'n derinnen I noticed his beautiful hand. Later that evening, as he helped me with the correct perspective on the gourd I was drawing, I noticed his wonderful scent. Thus as I join the ranks of those running from campus, I'm not quitting; I'm just heading to the mall for attractive new clothes to wear, black ones that will blend well with charcoal dust.

Being stuck on this man keeps me stuck on school while I figure out the thorny logistics of being a student again. Of course, there is the issue of how to make time for classes and homework, but the larger issue for me is how to deal with grades. When I attended college as a young adult, I was a neurotic student focused totally on getting A's. I figured that if I could study two hours, then I could study four. If I could study four hours, then I could study eight. My neurosis and study time increased exponentially. At the time, school was my whole life, and as focused as I was on A's, I never allowed myself to take classes at which I could not excel. But now I'm an adult with a full-time job, full-time family to monitor, full-time house to run, and full-time life, and I am taking classes about which I know nothing and in which I have no skills. While I recognize the potential to learn amazing new things, I also recognize the potential to earn awful grades in the process. Being an adult who is usually so capable, I find this thought difficult to bear.

It is very helpful to me, therefore, that my teacher is

a gentle and kind man. By this I mean that he does not laugh openly at any of my drawings. He also does not question the objects I group together in my still lifes done at home. My criteria for selection are things I think I can draw. He humors me by acting as though the world needs a charcoal rendering of a jug of bleach with containers of liquid Bold and Woolite all sitting on a flat surface with no hard-to-draw cloth underneath. Is it any wonder that I like him? I just can't wait to see what he thinks of my latest endeavor. There are three bottles of booze, two kinds of wineglasses, and a toy car all on that same flat surface. What makes this work so unique is its title: *This Class Is Driving Me to Drink.*

As kind and gentle as this man is in class, it remains to be seen if he can show rachmones in his grading. On my first three projects I got a B+, a B, and then a C+. I wonder if there is a pattern here and why I hear the echo of an old-time elevator operator shouting, "Going down." I also wonder what I should do about this issue. Perhaps all I can do is work on a new definition of success. The one I'm thinking of is this: I will consider myself a success if I attend every class, give an honest effort to every assignment, and make it through to finals week. Hmmm. Were I still into A's, I think this definition would earn me one in perspective.

After His Goodbye

I guess it would be an exaggeration to say that I am nursing a broken heart, as I only knew the man for eighteen days when he broke up with me. On the other hand, it is not an overstatement to say that I ache. As I review my current situation and reflect upon other times when I have been in this spot, I realize that there are many dynamics at work to explain my feelings. Of course, there is the fact that the potential for a significant partnership has been lost, but that's not the real problem for me. Instead, breaking up makes me doubt every aspect of my being. I seem to enter a new relationship with the thought that I have a lot to offer the guy and that he is lucky to have found me. By the time I have been ushered to the exit, however, I wonder if all my perceived plusses aren't minuses instead.

In this case, I "met" the man when he wrote me an e-mail message in response to an article I had written. Beyond the fact that I always respond to such letters, I was particularly interested in writing him because, in the space of his four-paragraph letter, he managed to reveal seven things about himself that were also true of me. With great gobs of chutzpah, I wrote him a letter in which I pointed out our similarities and suggested we pursue a friendship—unless, of course, his wife or girlfriend objected to the concept. Since there was no such woman in the picture, we began a correspondence and each wrote the other four long letters in which we mapped out our interests and personalities.

I know for a fact that I am an idiosyncratic person. I just happen to think that all of my foibles are darling and that they make me as cute as a button. Thus I told him in great detail and with glee about my propensity to cry at weddings, bar mitzvahs, consecrations, confirmations, nursery-school graduations, movies, the singing of the national anthem, and the sound of a Kenny G solo. I also told him with pride about my brand of intelligence, which does not include any knowledge of politics, world events, or geography. I probably even "boasted" that on a multiple-choice test I could pick out the names of all fifty states, but left to my own devices those same fifty names would not fall easily from my lips. The names of state capitals? Not a chance, but I'm a terrific researcher and I can locate that information in a snap.

I also mentioned my greatest strengths in life—I am a good friend, I am an empathic and supportive listener, and I dispense hugs with great regularity. I happen to think that all of these traits make me a wonderful specimen of womanhood, but obviously he did not. Instead of inviting me into his life with a *"kumt arein, bubeleh,"* he told me *"gai avek"* instead.

As I sit here nursing my pain and wondering if my darling idiosyncrasies aren't weird aberrations instead, I am comforted by a conversation I had with my seventeen-year-old daughter, Lisa. In telling me why a certain young man was her friend instead of her boyfriend, she explained that he always said her "something was too something"—her laugh was too loud, her teeth were too long, or her lips were too full. I can't fathom how anyone could say such things about my beautiful daughter. Of course, he's completely wrong about her laugh—it's rich and infectious. And he thinks her teeth are too long? Give me a break! And what's wrong with *him* that he doesn't notice the luscious nature of those amazing lips? Clearly, beauty is in the eye of the beholder, which is the lesson and salve I take from the conversation.

Reviewing my experience with the eighteen-day man, I often wonder which of my somethings he found too something. In the end, though, it doesn't matter how he filled in the blanks—by filling them in with negatives he proved he's not the one for me. Proceeding forward with Lisa's wisdom, I will only allow a man into my life if he can see me and fill in the blanks in a positive light. Short of that, I am prepared to say to future men what I now say to this one—"Back at ya with that goodbye!"

Cheetos, M&M's, and Rice Krispie Bars

When I get nervous I eat. A recent announcement from my friend Kathy has me firmly rooted in the kitchen. It seems that she and her steady beau, Michele (Me-kell-ay), have decided to sell their respective homes and buy a new one together. They have already placed a bid on a house and negotiations are under way. Kathy says that if living together works as well as they anticipate, marriage is next on the agenda. Were I the loving friend I wish I could be, her good news would fill me with nothing but delight. Instead, it is filling me with Cheetos, M&M's, and Rice Krispie bars as I egocentrically consider the impact of her actions on my life.

Kathy's news came via the phone, and even before our conversation ended, I was thinking about food. In fact, I worry that I was not effusive enough in my congratulations, so focused was I on what kind of *chozzerai* I might find in the pantry. After I hung up the phone, I headed to the kitchen, where I immediately recognized my nervousness and its source. I was afraid of losing Kathy's friendship as she committed herself to a love relationship. As I unwrapped my first Little Debbie Snack Cake, my other fear expressed itself—that I would never be so brave as to follow in her footsteps. Munching on my treat, I chewed these problems.

I am relatively new to the role of single woman. Since Kathy is the first of my friends to get married in my new life, I don't know what to expect after she says, "I do." It only seems logical, however, that girlfriends get bumped down a notch or two or three as a husband and his extended family enter the picture. Who needs a pseudofamily when they have the real thing? This makes all of my friendships with women feel precarious. Mary is smitten with Jim. Rose has two men in hot pursuit of her affections. Will I soon be left by all of these women? I am embarrassed to be so self-centered; yet this is the fear that has me *fressing*.

Speaking of eating, have I mentioned that I hate marshmallows? I do eat them, however, when I am desperate and have exhausted all other sweets in the house. The bag is open before me now as I consider the larger problem evoked by Kathy's announcement—my fear of living with a man on a full-time basis. This fear has two parts. The first one is as silly as it is troubling. When I divorced, my ex-husband kept the family home and almost everything in it, while I was given a settlement to purchase all that I needed for a new domain. After all these years in the new place, I still do not always have the right pot for a given recipe. Additionally, I am just to the point where I have accumulated extra hangers and a collection of rags. Were I to combine my possessions with someone else's and things did not work out, I am not certain I could bear being without hangers and *shmattes* again.

The second part of my concern is more important. Though I would try to invent a committed relationship that allowed me all the space I need for personal happiness, I'm not sure I could pull it off. I am reminded of an old acquaintance who announced that his wife was pregnant and boldly stated that the baby would not change their lives. They planned to take the baby along on all their museum outings, weekend trips, and the like. The marriage did not survive the reality of parenthood. I wonder if I could be more successful incorporating a husband into my life than they were with a baby.

It's been several weeks now since Kathy's announcement, and I find that I am still eating everything that's not nailed down because I just can't figure out this thing called marriage. I'm anxious, therefore, to see how Kathy and Michele negotiate their union. Of course, I hope that they will live happily ever after, but I hope these things for both altruistic and selfish reasons. I consider Kathy's action to be a brave and grand experiment, and, as if it were an epic motion picture on the big screen, I sit back now with popcorn and Coke in hand to watch it unfold, hoping to learn a lot.

The Banging of Pots

Here's a funky math problem for your consideration. On the Jewish calendar, the year 2000 is 5761. It's
interesting to note that on the Chinese calendar the
year is 4699 instead. The question, then, is this—what
do you get when you subtract 4699 from 5761? The
answer is the number of years that Jews have been without Chinese food at Christmas.

As another holiday season approaches, more questions arise than which restaurants are open on
Christmas Day. And so I ask, are you one of those people who feel blue in the weeks spanning Thanksgiving
to New Year's Eve? Do you watch friends scurry off to
dozens of parties while few invitations arrive in your
mail? And though you know "there's no place like
home for the holidays," do you feel more alone and
"single" than ever while you sit there within its walls? If
you answer yes to these questions, I have some simple
advice to offer—try something different this year.

My suggestion is to begin your own holiday traditions,

and though it takes years for such traditions to build, you will at least be on your way to happier holidays if you start now. Challenge yourself to add one new element to this year's Thanksgiving, one to this year's Chanukah, and one to this year's December 31 celebration. For instance, whom might you invite if you were to throw an open house during Thanksgiving weekend? What would it feel like to buy and wrap eight gifts for yourself at Chanukah? Wouldn't it be interesting to usher in the New Year in a different city? And on all of those holidays, wouldn't it be gratifying to volunteer at a nursing home or hospital?

It is important to keep a few things in mind as you construct holiday happiness. First, your actions this year are not to be done once and forgotten, but instead, they are to be the foundation for future years. Thus, if there are ten guests at your first open house, strive to have twelve at the second one. All year long, stash cash as you look forward to buying special gifts for yourself. Also, keep your ears open for interesting vacation spots as you add new cities to the list of those you've visited at the New Year.

As grand as all these plans sound, the second thing to remember is that the plans need not be grand at all. A very favorite tradition in our family is that I make fudge every year for the holidays. Half of the recipe gets served at Thanksgiving and the other half at Chanukah. We all salivate at the approach of the holiday season as we anticipate this favorite treat. New Year's Eve finds my kids and me out on the back deck banging pots with metal spoons at the stroke of midnight. It's cheaper and safer than shooting off fireworks and it's fun. And what about that idea of volunteering at a nursing home or hospital? It costs nothing and it's easy to arrange. Beyond that, it will help others and bear great gifts for the volunteer worker—an appreciation of being ambulatory, healthy, and able to live unassisted.

A final thing to keep in mind is that single folks are not the only ones to experience difficulties at this time of year. Let's face it; the season is hard for many—hard on the waistline, hard on the pocketbook, and hard on the emotions. There is so much hype for the holidays that there is bound to be disappointment. My dad once said of New Year's Eve that it is the most overrated night of the year. I think he's right, and expanding upon his wisdom, I think the whole holiday season is overrated. But since I am a member of this culture, there's no escaping it. I choose, therefore, to face it head on with a personal game plan for happiness as I revisit old holiday traditions and think of a few new ones to add to my repertoire.

It is said: "If you always do what you have always done, you will always feel what you have always felt." It is also said that insanity is doing the same thing over and over again expecting different results. Heeding these wise words, I say once again, to all who suffer from holiday blues: try something different this year. Start some new traditions. Bang a pot or two.

Tommy

I started dating Tom nine months ago and angrily broke up with him two months later. In spite of this fact, the guy just won't let me go. No, I don't mean that he is stalking me, nor is he phoning me incessantly to beg for my return. Instead, he's haunting me. His name whispers itself to me at odd moments of the day and night. I hear it as I awaken from sleep, as I pull laundry from the washer, as I take a loaf of bread from my grocer's shelf. I don't know why this is happening or how to make it stop. All I know is that like a fast-food hamburger repeating on me, my mind belches his name—"Tommy."

Though born a Catholic, Tom finds spirituality only in the physical movement of dance. Perhaps it's unfortunate, therefore, that I met him as I did, at a dance, at his most spiritual. When I saw him for the first time, there was a childlike look in his eyes of sheer joy. No, that's not right—it was something beyond joy. It wasn't ecstasy exactly. It was a quieter something, perhaps awe. I don't mean to imply that he was behaving in a spiritual or sedate manner, no, not Tom. In fact, he was dancing wildly, doing the Charleston to be precise, limbs flapping without restraint in striking contrast to his formal attire—black tuxedo complete with white gloves.

He was my date for the evening, a blind date arranged by my daughter. She lived away from home at the time, in a nearby college town, where he was a professor and her handsome next-door neighbor. The plan for our first date was to meet at a ball sponsored by his dance club. I was to ask for "Tom" and someone would point him out to me. That's how I came to lay eyes on him, the herky-jerky character with the spiritual glow. After his Charleston ended, we introduced ourselves. He then gave me a hurried lesson in the tango and led me to the dance floor, where he repeatedly changed his hold on my waist as he crisply turned me this way and that. At one point he dipped me low to the ground, raising his left eyebrow dramatically as he peered into my eyes and found terror there. Through his rakish grin he told me to relax, saying that he'd danced for ten years and never dropped a partner yet. He then continued to dance me around the floor with attitude and skill in great measure. It was amazing to be in the arms of a master.

In our two months "together," Tom and I had only five dates. There was the first one, when I saw him so clearly as a spiritual being, followed by two frustrating dates, when he refused to show that side at all or "let me in" emotionally. Holding out for the spiritual "prince" I met at the ball, I saw him for a fourth time.

We went to the ballet and then out to eat, and it was a magical evening. He said beautiful things to me, he took me in his arms and danced with me right there in the Olive Garden's dining room, and over dessert he gazed long and hard into my eyes. I thought we had turned a corner. But I was wrong. After that evening, his phone calls became short and less frequent, and on a fifth and final date he completely shut himself off to me. I wrote him an angry letter. He followed it with a phone call that made me madder still and that ended with a mutual agreement not to be in touch again. For seven months we have honored that agreement, except, of course, for the haunting.

Some may think that I hanker after Tom, but this is not the case at all. I want a man who allows his spirituality to shine through regularly, not sporadically. Thus the whisper of his name comes with annoyance, not longing. But why does it come and how do I make it stop? I surely do not know. Perhaps I'll search for an exorcist or some sort of Mylanta for the mind. Most likely, though, I'll just dance on with my life, being as graceful as possible whenever his whispered name chooses to "dip" me, as I wait for the day that Tom lets go of his hold and our "last tango in Ohio" comes to an end.

Scattering His Ashes

It was almost immediately after I fell for Kerry that he told me he was living with another woman. I would like to say that I was outraged and broke up with him on the spot, but that was not the case. I would like to say that he eventually decided to leave her for me, but that was not the case either. I would also like to say that in the fourteen months since I last saw the man, I have ceased wanting to be with him, but that's simply not the case. Though my logical mind knows that a man who plays around behind the back of one woman would certainly play around behind the back of the next, the simple truth is that the good things about the man were as terrifically wonderful as his infidelity was horrifically bad, and I sometimes still want him.

In my time with Kerry, songs played incessantly in my mind. A new one plays there now, supplanting the romantic ones. It's a parody of Bob Dylan—how many months will it take till I know this relationship just will not be? The answer, my friend, is blowing in the wind.

The answer is blowing in the wind. These words enter my mind with an inner knowing—it is time to close the door on thoughts of Kerry. In reality, I have been working toward this goal over the many months since I last saw him. Long ago I stashed photographs of him in my drawer, more recently I packed them away in a box with his letters, and for a good long time I have been thinking of some sort of ceremony to banish him from my thoughts.

I am reminded of a story I read in *Chicken Soup for the Soul*. It was written by Chick Moorman and told of a fourth-grade teacher who had her students take fifteen minutes to write down all the things they could not do in life. Each student wrote a page or more with statements such as: "I can't do long division with more than three numerals," "I can't hit one over the left-field fence," and "I can't do ten push-ups." When done, the students put their papers in a shoebox. The teacher then took the box, the kids, and a shovel out to the far corner of the playground, where she proceeded to bury the box. For the rest of the school year, the students were unable to say "I can't," because "I can't" was dead and buried in the schoolyard.

I would like this same kind of closure with Kerry. Instead of wanting to bury him, I am thinking of scattering his ashes, though murder is not part of the plan. During our time together, I broke up with him on two occasions over the issue of the other woman. Each time, he won me back with roses. As each bouquet died, I plucked the petals and displayed them on a heart-shaped dish. Those petals still sit on my kitchen counter. They are the last vestige of the man in my house, and they are the "ashes" I intend to scatter.

I live in the Midwest, and winter will soon be upon me. I plan to wait for a cold and windy day to sit in my backyard with my plate of petals and thoughts of Kerry. I will remember the first time I saw him. I will remember jumping up and down when he asked me out. I will remember his voice as he called me his darling girl. I will remember running my fingers through his hair and the curl that refused to stay down. I will remember buzzing around town in his little red convertible. I will remember all the restaurants and fine wine. I will sit there and remember it all for as long as it takes for the last rose petal to blow away, hoping that it takes a long time and that I get chilled to the bone in the process, so that I will also remember that his warm arms were never really available to hold me.

I ask myself, "Can I be done with him?" And with a happy song in my heart I respond, "The answer, darling girl, is blowing in the wind. The answer is blowing in the wind." Soon the last gust will carry away the last petal, and with it, the last longing for Kerry.

Reunion Revelation

After attending her fiftieth high-school reunion, my aunt Tillie wrote me a letter in which she said that all the "boys and girls" looked the same except that a few were using walkers. My aunt is currently ninety-one years old, so it's more than twenty years ago that I received her letter, but the humor of her comment has stayed with me. Moreover, as the decades pass and I attend reunion after reunion myself, I discover that her comment was also quite astute.

I had the opportunity at Thanksgiving to check out Aunt Tillie's observation once again, as I returned to my hometown of St. Louis to attend the reunion of U. City High School's Class of 1970. To be quite honest, I went there thinking that I had changed, that I had finally hit my stride, and that I was looking *good*—at last! It only took moments, however, to look around the room and see that each *boychik* and *maidel* looked like they did at eighteen—except, of course, for the gray hair and wrinkles—and thus to realize that the same must be true of me.

I was still reeling from this reality check and come-down, when Mike approached me. He was one of those really cool kids in high school, one who would not have spoken to bookish, studious me—not even to ask for class notes when he had missed a day—and here he was striking up a conversation. The single side of me looked immediately to his ring finger, but even finding a wedding band there, I was still intrigued to find out what this was all about, and so we spoke. In the course of our conversation I babbled on about how handsome he always was and how I had always admired him from afar and how I had giggled about him with my girl-friends and how I had written countless notes to them bearing his name. He smiled broadly at my words and told me something that I had forgotten. He said that I had approached him at our last reunion and told him the same things. The reason he had come up to me now was to tell me that my words had touched his heart.

A little bit of fireworks went off in my head to hear such a comment. Imagine that! Something *I* said affect-ed *his* life! Right on the spot I knew that his words had touched not only my heart but also my soul, as they gave me a wiser understanding of Aunt Tillie's com-ment about sameness. We chicks and boychiks not only look the same, we are the same. After thirty years, all the nerds, bookworms, and cool kids have melded into oneness, and we are at last on a level playing field.

Still glowing from his compliment and from the light it caused to go off in my head, I had the confi-dence to approach Debbie, another former classmate who had not only been ultracool as a teenager but who had seemed to have it all. As I chatted with this still beautiful woman, we compared the last ten years of our lives. I was heartbroken to learn how many tragic things had befallen her. Though I wouldn't wish all of her *umglick* on the devil himself, there was a good lesson to be learned from it. In further corroboration of my sameness theory, I learned that there are no charmed lives and that the continuous cycle of joy and pain affects us all.

I'm not sure why it took me so long to have this epiphany about sameness, as it was something I was taught as a junior at U. City High. The teacher was Mr. Lubeck, the class was American Studies, the topic of discussion was the Declaration of Independence, and the words were these: "We hold these truths to be self-evident, that all men are created equal." In my defense, I guess that I was always more of a mathematician than a historian, and so my mind was stuck in Mr. McSpadden's algebra class, thinking thoughts of less than and greater than instead. How lucky for me to finally learn the lesson now. I thank Mike and Debbie for the parts they played in my understanding, and I look forward to seeing both of these *friends* again at future reunions. And I wonder . . . what kind of revelations will come along with age spots and walkers in those years ahead?

The Bill Bobs

Embrace me, my sweet embraceable you. I am an attractive DWPF/NS, 48, 5' 7", 122 lb., who enjoys walking, bicycling, dancing, theater, reading, and long hours by the fire. I am self-employed, successful, intelligent, educated, creative, and sometimes lonely. ISO SWM 43-59 who is special. Please write.

There you have it, my personal ad as it appeared in *Cincinnati Magazine* last month. I placed it because as a singles columnist I feel compelled to go out on a date every once in a while and because as the ad says, I do get lonely at times. It's a little embarrassing to say that I placed the ad, but I have a secret to confess. I didn't just place one; I placed three. *Cincinnati Magazine* had a special—buy two, get one free—and I took advantage of it. Though I am a person who always looks for a bargain, the real reason I purchased three months of ads is that I am using the strategy espoused in *How to Find a Fella in the Want Ads,* by Zippy Larson. In that book, we are advised to systematically run ad after ad in order

122

to find our besherter. Larson tells us to vary the wording each time so as to appeal to different men. She says that by using this system, we will have loads of men from which to choose our true love. It sounded good enough to try, so I did.

The first month of my experiment has now ended and I have heard from six men—Bill, Bob, Bill, Bill, Bob, and Norm! On the one hand, I was disappointed by this response, having expected four times that amount. On the other hand, I have sometimes felt as if it is raining men, and I have been overwhelmed. Who's got time to explore six new friendships? Thus I have been forced to not only redefine a "good response rate" but also my method of dealing with potential new relationships. My normal modus operandi would be to take things very slowly, to write a few letters or make a few phone calls back and forth before meeting. But with six applicants for the position of boyfriend, I have found myself cutting to the chase and immediately suggesting a face-to-face encounter, remembering at all times that there are two more ads about to be published, which should bring even more Bill Bobs my way. Too many men is a wonderful problem to have, but just the same, *oy gevalt!*

Before describing each of my suitors, I should explain that my city magazine has two methods by which readers can respond to ads. They can call a 900 number to leave a voice-mail message, or they can send a letter to the magazine and have it forwarded. In my case, two voice-mail messages rolled in and then four letters. Caller number one was also letter writer number one, as he was so tsemisht that he did not realize he had contacted me twice. He also personified several traits that he abhorred in women. Since I do not believe in double standards, I crossed that Bill off my list twice. Bob number one also phoned. He sounded like a fun guy and I particularly enjoyed learning that he had once been a musician in a clown band. However, he made it abundantly clear that he wanted someone of his own religion, which I was not, thus I did not return his call. That left one Bill, one Bob, and Norm. As per Bill's request, I have written him and now await his next letter. Bob and I have a date later this week, and I have had three meals with Norm. He is a handsome, highly educated man who owns a hardware store, making him a dream come true for an unhandy woman such as myself. But there's always a "but," and this is his—even though he is very fond of kissing me, he's not comfortable with the fact that we are of different religions.

I must confess that I am eager to see what happens with these men and with future respondents. I must also confess that I have had a sneak preview in that regard. Ad number two hit newsstands six days ago, and between the two ads I have had eight more responses. What can I say? When it rains it pours! *Oy gevalt and geshrigen!* This experiment sure seems to have potential!

Recommending a Kodak Moment

There's no accounting for personal taste. I learned this important lesson at my square-dance club, in a conversation with my buddy Sam. We were talking about two women present that night who happened to be sisters and about the odd fact that one was so attractive while the other was so plain. Astoundingly, though, the one I found unappealing was the beautiful one in his eyes. Intrigued, I then asked Sam to look around the room and tell me whom else he found attractive and was again shocked by his response. The down side of this experience was that it erased all those many compliments he had paid me over the years, while the up side was to teach me that beauty is indeed in the eye of the beholder.

I bring this up now because I would like to state an opinion that will not be popular. For those singles who sometimes answer personal ads, I think it best if you include a photograph of yourself with your first letter. Yes, yes, I know, you don't photograph well. And I know

you really are going to lose a few pounds or change
your hairstyle between the time you send the letter and
the other person responds, but just the same, I vote for
sending the photo.

This opinion is born of personal experience. I am
currently running the second of three personal ads in
a local magazine. Though I did not ask men to include
a photo with their response, I have been surprised and
greatly pleased on the three occasions when they have
done so, and these are the men I have contacted first.
Please do not think that all of these men have been
drop-dead gorgeous, because they were not. However,
I liked very much the confidence level they exhibited
by sending a photograph. Additionally, having a photo
helps me in two ways. When I only know a man's
height, weight, and hair color, I tend to run into other
men with these same specs who look as if they have
escaped from the state penitentiary or mental institu-
tion. A photo in hand can therefore dispel a lot of
doubts. It can also decrease the embarrassment level of
the first meeting, as I don't have to approach every
man who walks into the rendezvous spot and feel as if
I'm coming on to him as I virtually ask, "Hey baby,
lookin' for me?"

As you consider showing the other person what you
look like in your introductory letter, please keep in
mind that beauty is a very subjective thing. There is
no definitive answer to the question, who is *mees* and
who is *shain*? If you could have an "eye transplant"
and see yourself as your friends do, you'd probably be
impressed with the view. If, however, you really are a
zhlub or a *shlumper*, then it's time to clean up your act.

Get a new haircut and put on some clean clothes, for goodness sake! Then, putting your best foot forward, hold your head high and snap a new photo. Yes, I said a new one. No one cares what you looked like ten or twenty years ago. Be proud of the current you, remembering at all times that you were created in God's image, so how bad can that be?

In a further attempt to sell the idea of sending a photo, let me tell you about two men I have met through my ads. If we were to put Man A and Man B through the swimsuit and evening-wear competition of a beauty pageant, I believe that almost everyone would vote for Man A—except of course for my buddy Sam. But I'll tell you, even though Man B is not half as handsome as Man A, his looks call out to me loud and long because he resembles a man I once loved and lost. To borrow from the vernacular, is he a hunk? No. To borrow from Elvis, is he a hunk a hunk of burning love? He just might be. In my mind he is certainly worthy of further exploration, even if he does come in last in the beauty contest.

This brings us back to the start—there is no accounting for personal taste—and to the opinion that it is a good idea to include a photo when you answer a personal ad. In my book, it's time for a Kodak moment.

The Blond
Gwyneth Paltrow

Ten years ago, I attended my high-school reunion and had the opportunity to chat with an old boyfriend, Ben Wildman. My daughter was with me at the time, and when I introduced them, she asked him in typical seven-year-old style, "What if my mommy had married you? Would my name be Wild Woman?" It was hard to explain to Lisa all the implications of that particular "what if," not the least of which was the fact that she would not exist. It was also interesting to contemplate the hundreds—or would it be thousands?—of ways in which my life would be different had I made that particular choice.

For anyone who has ever taken a flight of fancy to consider the "what ifs" of their own life, I recommend an interesting movie available on video. It is an English film called *Sliding Doors*, starring Gwyneth Paltrow, John Hannah, and John Lynch. Paltrow plays the part of Helen, a single woman who works at a public-relations agency to support herself and Gerry, her live-in boyfriend, who is a writer. The movie opens on the morning that Helen gets fired at work. As she dejectedly leaves the office and walks to the subway to return home, she has the additional misfortune of missing her train. We watch with her as its doors slide shut moments before she can get through them. While all of this is happening to Helen, Gerry is at home having an affair with his ex-flame. Had Helen caught her subway, she also would have caught them. At this point, screenwriter and director Peter Howitt asks "what if" and proceeds to give us the parallel stories of Helen's life down both paths.

The thing that I liked most about the two stories of her life was that they were both very plausible. In neither life did the screenwriter have Helen win a lottery, inherit a million dollars, or get discovered as a superstar. Instead, he showed us the large impact of the small decisions she actually made, making this a movie from which we can all learn.

In the story in which Helen missed her train, she stays with Gerry and works two low-paying jobs to support him—delivering sandwiches to offices by day and waitressing by night. In this tale, Helen is too tired to care about her looks, and wears her mousy brown hair in two braided pigtails. In the companion story, she leaves Gerry after discovering his infidelity and moves in with a girlfriend who encourages her to get a new image, which includes short, frosted blond hair. The friend also prods her to pursue James, a man she met when she made it through the sliding doors of the train. It is James who suggests to Helen that she think of opening her own PR firm. Applying for a small-business loan, she does just that. In this version we watch a blond, beautiful, and confident woman strike out on her own to make the most of her many talents.

The screenwriter does an excellent job of untwisting the two stories and bringing us back to an acceptable reality at the end. As a matter of fact, as the movie concluded, I might have broken into a huge round of applause over his clever handling of the plot, except for the fact that I was running for my journal to write the following note: "I want to be the blond Gwyneth Paltrow!" By this I mean that I want to always put my best foot forward in regard to my physical appearance, I want to have faith in myself professionally, and I want to have the courage to recognize and walk away from dead-end relationships.

All of these are obtainable goals that, combined, would have great impact. The beauty of this film, then, is that it not only looks into the past to ask "what if", but also encourages us to apply the "what if" question to the future. Life is a Robert Frost poem, and there are countless junctures where "two roads [diverge] in a yellow wood." Obviously our choices, even the seemingly small ones, determine the course of our lives. Keeping this in mind, we can strive to make empowering choices, ones that speak to our higher selves, ones that allow us to become the blond Gwyneth Paltrow.

Waiting for Gedult

Back in November of 2000, I saw a road sign that caused my blood to chill. It said, *Road Construction Thru December 2001 Delays Possible at Times.* Thinking immediately of highway signs that mention construction for the next ten miles and all the obstacles that that entails, I immediately imagined fourteen months of traffic jam before I could get home. I felt sick. And impatient. And ready to laugh hysterically until I cried. For you see, I am a person who is always on shpilkes, and gedult is something I possess in short supply.

They say that patience is the ability to count down before blasting off. They say that patience is the knowledge that you must travel through the wilderness before you can make it to the Promised Land. They also say that patience is the understanding that you cannot sow and reap on the same day. I don't know who "they" are, but I'm not one of them. What I say instead is, "Nu?!", "Nu *shoyn!*", and *"Shoyn genug!"*

This impatience is apparent in all areas of my life.

When a restaurant tells me that the wait is fifteen minutes, I immediately set my stopwatch for that time and begin bouncing my knee one second after reaching it. Additionally, my children will tell you that when a home-cooked dinner is slated for 6:30, I don't mean 6:31. And there are even a few policemen out there who could tell you about my impatience with posted speed limits when I am in a rush. These are the guys, though, who have made me understand that my hurried nature can lead to trouble.

I have come to realize that my speed-demon tendencies have caused problems in my male/female relationships too. There was that one guy, for instance, with whom I had an e-mail correspondence. We wrote long letters back and forth in which we shared all sorts of tidbits of our lives and in which we debated the merits of remaining pen pals or meeting in the flesh. I was the one driving for a face-to-face meeting and, with my foot firmly set on that gas pedal, I drove the relationship right into a brick wall. It wasn't until months later that I realized the entire friendship had lasted eighteen days. What was my hurry? I guess I was dealing with a tankful of loneliness, and I didn't know it was so combustible.

In his book, *What Men Won't Tell You But Women Need to Know,* Bob Berkowitz comments on this topic. He says, "Commitments aren't instant pudding. If the relationship is going to gel it will take longer than five minutes." Trying to have a *bisseleh* patience, I wonder, what does this mean—six?

The man with whom I am impatient at the moment is named Bob. We met as a result of my personal ad and had several phone conversations followed by a date for coffee. As we left the restaurant, we both confessed to having a good time and even hugged in parting. A week passed and he did not call. Since I could have sworn we had a good time, I wrote him. I suggested two reasons why he might not have gotten back to me. One was that he was waiting to hear from me and the other was that he was uninterested in a friendship. In case it was the former, he had now heard from me. In case it was the latter, I told him not to reply and I'd get the hint. He called immediately and excitedly upon receiving his mail to say he was interested but busy. He said he'd call me when he could. That turned out to be three weeks later. I wasn't home, so he left me a voicemail message, and then I left him one in turn. Days have passed. Could it be six—or maybe seven? What's this girl to do now—have patience?

They say that a handful of patience is worth more than a bucketful of brains. They say that many a man has turned and left the dock just before his ship came in. They say you can accomplish almost anything with patience. You can even carry water in a sieve if you wait for it to freeze. They also say that good things come to those who wait. And so I am waiting—waiting for gedult.

Machetunim?
Mishpoche? Meshugeh?

Am I completely crazy or is this odd? Here's what happened: I had a lot of out-of-towners come to Cincinnati over the winter holiday. There was my son, Scotty, who was visiting from New York with his beautiful girlfriend, Cheryl. There was my daughter Shana, who was visiting from San Diego with her handsome honey, Scotty B. There were my folks, who came from St. Louis to see the kids, and let's not forget Jet, my ex-boyfriend, who has known and loved my kids for six years and who came in from Indiana for the same purpose. As I continue to describe the scene, you'll need to know that my folks still have a lovely relationship with my ex-husband and they go out with him at least once whenever they come to town. And so it came to pass that he stopped by my house to pick them up. In the midst of all the happy hellos, I witnessed the oddity—my ex-husband and ex-boyfriend in an embrace, slapping each other on the back as they excitedly exclaimed, "How ya doin', buddy? Long time no see!"

I looked around for some sort of Jewish mistletoe to explain the occurrence, but finding none, I just had to scratch my head and wonder.

The oddness carried over to the next day as well. Though both of my children spent several days in town, there was only one twenty-four-hour period in which their visits overlapped. Their dad wanted to have them for dinner that night, as did I, so we compromised and broke bread together in a restaurant. All of the above-mentioned people were there plus three others: my younger daughter, Lisa, her stepmother, and her step-sister. Hold on to your hats, because in the next round of happy helloing, Jet hugged my ex-husband's new wife while her twenty-five-year-old daughter hugged me. Through the whole bizarre experience, my inner voice was shouting, "Vos iz dos?"

What is this indeed? Well, it's the wonderful world of divorce in the early 2000s. And we are a group of people bound together by a love for three children—Scott, Shana, and Lisa—and by a desire to make the best of an awkward situation for the sake of those children.

In case it isn't already abundantly clear, I will confess that I am conflicted by our behavior. What my head knows is good is not yet felt in my heart, so I try to explain it to myself, try to give our group a name in order to validate it. *Machetunim* comes to mind, though it's a group of people related through marriage and we are a group united by divorce. *Mishpoche* also comes to mind. It's a family including the remotest of kin. But while a cousin three times removed may be a part of the group, I doubt that a spouse "once removed" by a court of law is. Next, I think that like "Jews by Choice," we have all chosen to be part of this particular tribe, and then I laugh at myself for such a notion. We are divorced, after all, and do not wish to be kinsmen at all. It occurs to me finally that my ex and I are two people who just happen to be members of the large group of people our children call family, with me on their mother's side and he on their father's and never the twain shall meet. And then I laugh at myself again and say, "Methinks the lady protests too much." Despairing of ever finding a name for us, I put away my game of semantics.

Unable to get my heart to understand the situation, I disengage it for now and turn back to my logical mind, which knows that by any name we call this hugging mass of humanity, it is wise—for the sake of my children—to be a part of it. Therefore, even though I sometimes feel that I should be awarded a military medal for courage—or at least be given a boatload of chocolate—after one of our little get-togethers, I will say with all honesty that as odd, meshugeh, and unbelievable as this all seems to me, I am proud and pleased that we are behaving in this manner.

Bring on the next hugger—and a couple pounds of chocolate to boot!

Fishing

Whenever I suffered a broken heart as a teenager, my best friend's mom would tell me that there were a lot of fish in the sea. It helped to know this, but it would have helped even more if she had told me how to land one. It is now thirty years later and I think I have finally figured out a way to play this particular game of "Go Fish." The answer lies in running personal ads. Here are the main rules of the game: run ad after ad in whatever publication you choose, vary the ad monthly, then wait for the results to swim in.

I made a three-month commitment to this plan, choosing my city magazine as the publication whose demographics best suited my needs. At the end of the first month, my ad had garnered six responses. The magazine's policy is to forward letters for six months. Thus now, at the end of the second month, my first ad has had five more responses while my second ad has had eleven of its own. Some of the same men responded to both ads, so I didn't really hear from twenty-two men; it was only sixteen instead. But for me, a woman who is not a voluptuous, curvaceous, knock-'em-dead gorgeous kind of girl, this constitutes a pretty amazing school of fish.

For those who wonder what I may have said to receive such a response, I merely spoke from my heart. The most difficult part of being single for me is dealing with home repair, and thus in my current ad I wrote the following:

Hey there, SWPM/NS 43-59, do you have seams in need of repair? Buttons that fell off? Hungry for home cooking? Then write me, an attractive DWPF/NS 48, 5' 7", 123 lb., with light bulbs up high that need changing. Let's help each other, laugh with each other, and proceed from there.

You will notice that the ad is relatively short. This is because you pay by the word for these ads, because most people have a short attention span when reading them, and because even if I wrote a thousand words, I could only convey a thimbleful of who I am. Additionally, I didn't give a long list of what I am looking for in a man because I demand to be myself in a relationship and must extend the same right to him. Also, I believe that good men come in all shapes, sizes, and guises.

For those who wonder if I have attracted any good men through this process, the answer is a definite yes. With the exception of one respondent—who wanted to change my light bulbs and light my fire—the worst thing I can say about these guys is that some of them are desperately lonely and some of them think they are taller than in fact they are. The best I can say is that I am currently dating two of them. One is a handsome man who has an MBA from Vanderbilt and who owns his own business. The other is a very tall, very successful tax attorney for a big-name firm who is planning to take a year off to explore the West Coast. Whether or not either of these guys proves to be my true love is anyone's guess, but they are substantial, good people, and not the wackos or perverts that some expect to find through the personals.

Though it's amazing for me to be dating two nice guys at the same time, the truly phenomenal thing about this personal-ad game plan is that, indeed, there is always another fish in the sea waiting to be reeled in. If I go out with a new guy who's not right for me, I don't have to ache with disappointment. If I go out with a guy who is rude in any way, I don't have to put up with it. If I go out with a guy whom I like but who doesn't return the feelings, I don't have to be crushed by his rejection. I just go home and call the next man.

I have never had men lined up for the opportunity to be with me, nor has the phone ever rung off the hook in that regard. Thus I find this to be quite exciting and empowering, and for now, I'm sold on personal ads hook, line, and sinker.

Wanted: Tuesdays
with Lorie

For more than three years now, Mitch Albom's book, *Tuesdays with Morrie,* has spent time on the bestseller list. In case you somehow missed it, the story is this—Morrie Schwartz was a doctor of sociology at Brandeis University and Mitch was his student there. While taking every course the professor offered, Mitch struck up a friendship with Morrie, which included informal gabfests on Tuesdays. When Mitch graduated, he pledged to stay in touch but failed miserably to do so. Fate intervened years later to bring the men back together as Morrie lay dying from Lou Gehrig's disease. With Tuesday meetings reestablished, Morrie teaches Mitch a final course—The Meaning of Life.

My favorite part of the book is at the end, when Morrie announces that he has selected the site at which he will be buried. He tells Mitch that it is on a hill, beneath a tree, overlooking a pond. He says it's very serene and a good place to think, and he suggests that Mitch come there on Tuesdays to visit him and to continue to share his problems. Mitch is taken aback by this idea until Morrie explains that Mitch can still talk and Morrie will still "listen."

Most people would take this to mean that cemeteries are peaceful places to go when life's problems require reverie, and as we go there to find our answers, the remembered voices of our dearly departed can help guide us. But that's only a part of what I heard in Morrie's words. Being a single person, I also read this as Morrie's plan for companionship at the grave, and I found it to be so compelling that it caused me to concoct my own. Instead of a "room with a view" to entice visitors, here's what I've come up with—I want the only word on my gravestone to be *MOM*. I want no birth date or date of death to be shown, for I do not wish to be a specific mom, but instead, the generic. That way, every person in the human race can come visit me, and I will be loved and not lonely through eternity, even though my plot is a single one and not double.

I joke a little in saying this and yet I mean it quite sincerely, as this plan solves two thorny problems for me. As for most people, thoughts of my own demise have always been troubling, but there are a couple of twists to my situation. While married, my ex and I left our hometown in our early twenties and never returned. As corporate gypsies, we then moved around a lot. I always wondered, therefore, where I'd end up when it came time for burial, and who, if anyone, would visit my grave in that foreign city. Yes, I know my kids will visit, but what if they learned what they lived and become gypsies too? Then who will come?

Additionally, there is the problem of my name.

When I divorced, I kept my married name in order to have a link to my children. Though I am glad I did this, I have no desire to go through all of eternity with the weight of that named engraved on my tombstone. Death, however, would be an odd time to take back my maiden name, and only Cher can get away with using a first name alone. Since the role of mother has been my greatest joy in life, the word *MOM* seems an appropriate way to label my remains and a perfect solution to my problems.

Please forgive me for having such grave thoughts, but I write these words in the wee hours of the morning in a hospital room as I watch my dear friend, Jet, sleep after undergoing angioplasty to clear a 90 percent blockage in his heart. I also write them as I honor the *yortzeit* of my beautiful friend, Jo, who died of cancer two years ago. Thus I know from experience that any course on "The Meaning of Life" must also include the topic of death. As Mitch Albom indicates, for all of us students of life, "a funeral [will be] held in lieu of graduation." The upside to thinking these thoughts is an understanding of Morrie's final lesson. He said, "Once you learn how to die, you learn how to live."

Rest in peace, Morrie. Rest in peace, Jo. *Zei gezunt,* Jetty.

Long ago when my kids were little, there was a segment on "Sesame Street" that spoke to me. In it, a Wild West cowboy burst into a saloon brandishing a gun and hollering, "I wanna know why!" Having shouted those very same words at the heavens on more than one occasion, I immediately perked up as I waited with him for an answer. Unfortunately, it turned out that he was inquiring about the letter *Y,* and so I never got the answer to what I had hoped was the question—why is life so difficult?

Since "Sesame Street" let me down, I have turned to alternate sources over the years for possible answers, and I have finally found a guy who seems to have some. He is the well-known author, Kurt Vonnegut. My introduction to his work was his 1997 book, *Timequake.* On page one he mentioned that his mother and sister found life to be unbearable. On page two he quoted Mark Twain saying much the same thing. This page also included Henry David Thoreau's quotation, "The mass of men lead lives of quiet desperation." Since page one also contained Vonnegut's belief that the mission of an artist is to make people appreciate being alive, I felt hopeful that he had some answers for those of us who struggle.

In the course of reading this book and an earlier one, *Slaughterhouse Five*, I have learned many things about Vonnegut that make me even more confident of his status as an answer man. At age seventy-eight, he has experienced much in life. He served in World War II. He was taken prisoner at the Battle of the Bulge. And as a POW, he experienced the bombing of Dresden, in which more people died than Hiroshima. His more "mundane" struggles have included the loss of his mother to suicide, the loss of his sister to cancer when she was forty-one, and the demise of a twenty-two-year marriage to his childhood sweetheart. In spite of his *gehakteh tsores*, the man doesn't shout at the heavens but instead finds a lot of joy in life, in such things as good books, jazz, and petting his second wife's *tochis*.

As it turns out, Vonnegut's books are jam-packed with his beautiful way of looking at life. One of my favorite parts of *Timequake,* for example, was when he discussed his writing style. He uses a manual typewriter, makes corrections in pencil, and then sends his pages off to a woman for retyping. Since neither he nor the typist own fax machines, he sends them via the mail. This necessitates having an envelope and stamps and causes him to spend much time visiting stationery stores and the post office. Vonnegut's wife suggests he buy a thousand envelopes to keep on hand. Though he knows this would be practical, it's not the point, for

Vonnegut believes "we are here on Earth to fart around."

Another valuable lesson in the book came as Vonnegut discussed his uncle Alex, who said that when things are going well, we should be sure to notice. He was talking about the simple occasions in life, not the grand victories. Thus when we notice the scent of baking bread, or the taste of cold lemonade on a hot afternoon, we should remember to exclaim, "If this isn't nice, what is?" Yes, I know we have all heard this before, but we need to hear it again, because it seems that the answers in life really are quite simple. It's just believing that they are the answers that is so hard.

Vonnegut even has an explanation for male/female difficulties. Other men may not know what women want, but Vonnegut does—they want a whole lot of people to talk to. As for men, they need a bunch of men with whom to share their dumb jokes. He says that the divorce rate is so high today because of the demise of the extended family. When you get married nowadays, all you get is one person and that's simply not enough.

Why is life difficult? After only two Vonnegut books, I have many answers, and here are a few—because we forget to fart around, because we forget to focus on the nice moments, and because we don't have enough people around us to share all the bad jokes of life.

For years I've shouted to the heavens, and at last there is a reply. Kurt Vonnegut: astute, funny, and wise. Yippee-yahoo!

Kaboom

I think I've struck each of my kids once in their life-time. In each case it was a *potch* on a diaper-padded tushie. Thus when they mouth off at me and I say, "Watch out or I'll pop you in the nose," they know this is a figure of speech that I use and has nothing to do with a threat of physical violence. Instead, it means something along the lines of, "You better calm down now—you're making me meshugeh." Likewise, when a bunch of teenage girls recently did something to hurt my daughter and I told her that I wished I had a sub-machine gun to mow them all down, she did not call a S.W.A.T. team or a group of terrorist negotiators. Instead, she understood that I, too, ached with the pain of their actions and was merely venting.

Years ago, I made a statement of this sort when one of my kids' friends was visiting our home. Since that child did not know me very well, he was unable to decode my meaning. Taking my words literally, there-fore, he looked at me with suspicion and fear. From this experience I learned that there is a lot of room for misunderstanding in the spoken word. Other life experiences have taught me that this is doubly true for the written one.

All of this knowledge rattled around in my brain as I recently dealt with Darryl, a man I dated a half-dozen times after meeting him through a personal ad. All right, I admit, it, I did something sort of awful to hurt his feelings. After the incident we had a long phone conversation as we tried to mend fences. A week later he sent me a letter that outlined all his emotions on the issue and included an apology for his end of the squabble. In our phone conversation I evidently told him that I differ so much from the women he usually dates that I feared he'd "just blow me off" one day. In his letter he said, "There may be one bit of humor in all this. You mentioned that I might just 'blow you off.' . . . What I'd rather do is **<u>BLOW YOU UP!</u>** (Watch where you leave your car.) Just kidding."

It wasn't until I read the letter for a third time that it occurred to me that this statement might be a threat, and though I didn't exactly feel fear, I did feel some uneasiness over his capitalized and underlined words, not to mention his exclamation point. This emotion was heightened that evening when my garage-door opener suddenly went on the fritz and I had to park my car in the driveway instead of the locked garage overnight. It was heightened even further when I drove my car the next day and had a problem with the engine dying. Though I chuckled over my good luck that it was the engine that died and not me, I wondered if all my malfunctioning machinery was a coincidence or the plotting of a madman.

I turned to my friend Roberta with that question. I told her Darryl seemed like a nice guy. He seemed nonviolent. He had never said or done anything to alarm me. But even as I listed his many fine personality traits, I made jokes about my car going "kaboom." I also made sure I gave Roberta Darryl's name, address, and phone number just in case it did. Yes, I was worried, because here's what I figured out—when becoming involved with a man who is a virtual stranger, it is possible to know the taste of his lips without knowing the flavor of his soul.

Talking to Darryl about this was certainly an option, but I feared doing so. What if he became inflamed to hear my suspicions about him? What if he laughed diabolically to confirm them? In the end, though, he called me and we had the opportunity to talk things out. It turns out that he really is the fine guy I thought him to be. Thus we had a good laugh over his unfortunate choice of words and over my quasi-panic.

It's a relief to know that Darryl doesn't really want to blow me up but instead merely wants to pop me in the nose and/or mow me down with a submachine gun. Whew! I sure got lucky this time. *Danken Got.*

Pleading the Fourth

Published author and columnist now wants to write a romance. ISO SWPM/NS 43-59 who wants to star in the male role. As the female lead, I am a successful, attractive, happy DWPF/NS 48, 5' 7", 123 lb. who enjoys all the finer things in life and the simple ones as well.

What do you think? Great personal ad, eh? I sure thought so. Or why would I have put out good money to have it printed? As it turns out, though, it was a dud. I have run three consecutive ads and have changed the wording monthly. This one had the worst response rate. Only six guys contacted me as compared to eleven on my first ad and twelve on the next. In all honesty, it hurt like crazy to suffer the rejection of so few responses—that is, until I sat myself down and gave myself a talking to. "Hey, Cutie Pie," I said, "there are two parts to consider here, the ad and the person behind the ad. The words used to describe the person might have stunk but the person is still stellar." It is exactly for this reason of inadvertently bad ad copy that single folks should run different ads when playing the personals.

Another lesson learned from this three-month experiment of mine is that if played with serious intent, this is a time-consuming game that takes some organizational skills. In my town there seems to be a profusion of Bills, Bobs, Mikes, and even Norms. Since most of these guys give only their first names in their initial contact, it is hard to keep them straight without a scorecard. Thus I developed a spreadsheet to manage my men. Reviewing it now and adjusting for those men who responded to more than one of my ads, I see that I heard from twenty different guys. With the exception of three, all of them seemed interesting enough for me to write or phone. At this point I have found the time to contact twelve of them, eight of whom I went on to meet with varying degrees of success. A couple of these men are still lingering in my life, and of course, there is that handful of guys that I have yet to contact.

I should describe the three I rejected without even phoning. One wanted a "good Christian woman," which I obviously am not. The second wrote in a manner that was slightly lewd. And the third was far too pushy. Respondents to my city's magazine can choose to write a letter or leave a voice-mail message on a special 900 telephone line. This man left a message telling me—not asking me—to call him ASAP. He then called back the next day sounding huffy over the fact that I did not. I should note that this man had a heavy foreign accent, so maybe our difficulties were cultural in nature. But even putting that aside, I was not interested in meeting him—I have so much difficulty understanding men who speak English that it seemed unwise to pursue one with a foreign tongue.

Regarding the men I actually went out with, I recognize fully that I date myself in describing them, but in the first batch there was a Perry Como lookalike, in the second batch an Arnold Palmer twin, and in this last go-round someone who looked Captain Kangaroo-ish. The questions are these: is the situation improving or deteriorating, and how many batches must there be before a Robert Redford ringer comes along?

The upside to all of this dating is that practice makes perfect, and I am now quite comfortable with meeting new men. The downside is that I am becoming overwhelmed with disappointment. It would be nice to come home from one of these dates smitten. Head over heels in love—or lust—would be nice. But this has just not been the case. Thus, after playing around with personal ads through all of November, December, and January, I have dated myself into an exhausted funk. In the back of my mind, a corollary to the Fourth Commandment calls out to me saying, "Three months shalt thou labor and do all thy dating but the fourth month is the time to rest, regroup, and rethink things." I listen to this wise whispering of my soul and say amen.

It's time to focus on girlfriends for a while.

Equal but Opposite Prejudices

I would like to tell the story of a man who will remain nameless. You will soon see why. Nameless is a man I dated half a dozen times. He was born and raised a Southern Baptist in a tiny town in southeastern Kentucky. As an adult he is a highly educated Methodist living in Cincinnati. From the start he had difficulties with the fact that I am a Jew. If truth be told, he had dual concerns. He wondered why I would want to be with him and why he would want to be with me. If you question why we chose to be together, then, please keep in mind a little thing called "chemistry," which is God's way of making a man and woman hang out together long enough to get to know each other.

Nameless is a guy with a great memory. He can remember every stop he made on a car trip taken ten years ago, classroom discussions of all the literature he read in college, and a college discussion he had on the Jews. The question under consideration was this: are Jews a religion or a race? The answer derived that day was that we are a race. Thus for Nameless, dating me was an interracial experience, and he struggled so with this concept that he sometimes made me feel as if he was not just dating outside of his religion and/or race, but also outside of his species.

On our third date, for example, he pushed back from the restaurant table and said apropos of nothing, "I can't believe that I didn't think about it once during dinner." Of course, I asked, "Think about what?" And his answer was, "That I'm eating with a Jew." My friend said she would have replied, "And I can't believe that I am eating with a bigot." But you see, I didn't feel that way at all. Open-mindedness is a relative thing, and for a man with his upbringing, he was being very open-minded, and getting more so with every passing moment. Thus I just laughed at him and told him how awful his words sounded. "What am I," I asked, "an orangutan?" Of course, I also told him that had he been eating with any other Jewish woman he would be wearing his leftovers instead of taking them home in a doggie bag.

Now as you're no doubt feeling huffy over Nameless's words—and certainly understanding why I felt he needed the protection of being nameless—let me tell the second part of this story. Two days after this dinner, I got a letter from one of my readers, who was upset over the fact that I choose to date non-Jews. The letter was written in a very caring and loving tone, but it went on nonetheless to tell me that to date a non-Jew—and to encourage others to do so through my example—was against Jewish law and tradition. The writer closed by saying that she hoped I would soon find enough Jewish pride to think it unbearable to inter-date.

I found the juxtaposition of this letter and my date with Nameless to be quite startling. He thought it unbelievable to be with a Jew, while she thought it unbearable to be with a non-Jew. As for me, I felt blasted by both sides. In my mind two questions begged asking—aren't these equal but opposite prejudices, and aren't we all God's children worthy of love?

I believe that the problem with organized religion is that it divides people. I personally do not believe that there is one true religion, though I do believe that there is one true God. Therefore, I don't care by what name another person calls God, just as long as that person chooses to be in touch with Him.

Feeling as I do, I have no choice but to respect Nameless, the lady who wrote me, and even myself as we struggle in our own ways to figure out the unknowable and live spiritual lives. I also respect the Reform Judaism of my upbringing, because it gave me a "live and let live" attitude toward people of different religions and afforded me the room to question these things. I am extremely proud to be such a Jew, proud to be a person who has God in my life.

Flat Tires

I once read a short story that said a woman with a flat tire had two options. She could either call AAA or the suicide prevention hotline. Yes, I know that some women can change a tire, and I'm very proud of them, but I'm simply not one of them. Thus I laughed in painful recognition at this line. My own ineptitude is born of the fact that I was pampered in regard to cars for most of my life. Until I was twenty-one, my dad took care of all insurance, maintenance, washing, waxing, and tank-filling tasks. My husband carried on with those duties until I separated from him at forty. These guys also handled fender benders and blowouts. During those years, when I got a flat tire, I'd call my main man, who in turn called AAA for me. I liked this system.

While I am proud to say that taking on the responsibility of a car at the age of forty did not push me over the edge, I also must admit that it was a challenge. My son, Scott, took me to the gas station for a lesson in pumping gas, and though I caught on quickly, I was dismayed when the next service station had an entirely different nozzle and start mechanism. He also convinced me that I had the capability and courage to drive through the local car wash, but he never mentioned that other ones had a tricky track that I would have to fit my tires on in order to be pulled through the system. After a few embarrassments in these endeavors, I was less than enthusiastic when he next suggested that I learn a little about cars so that I could hold my own with mechanics.

It was at this point that I developed what has become my mantra, saying then what I say now—"I know nothing about cars and I wish to know nothing about cars." I choose to forgive myself completely for this disinterest and ignorance. As I see it, there are lots of things in life that I know nothing about, and if I had the time to learn a new skill, I'd take up the piano, not auto mechanics. Thus, when it comes to my own vehicle, all I know is its year, make, model, and color. Cylinders? Yes, it probably has some, but it could have turbo jets too for all that I know or care.

So what's a single woman who feels this way supposed to do? Well, I had a great idea for a man who is looking to start his own business. He could rent himself out to single women, divorcées, and widows to take care of all those things that men are supposed to take care of, meaning home repair, lawn care, snow shoveling, and, in this case, car maintenance. Unable to find a man to open the first Husbands 'R Us, though, I did the next best thing. I chose a car dealership to use exclusively. Their computer keeps track of all scheduled maintenance and sends me little reminders at appropriate times.

When I make an appearance at their shop, I repeat my mantra as I tell them to do whatever it takes to keep my car humming. My Scotty plotzes to hear this, fearing these guys will take advantage of me. Understanding fully that any extra cost is just the expense of husband rental, I tell him, "Frankly, my dear, I don't give a d—."

Last week I had an appointment at the dealership. I told the service manager that all I needed besides an oil change was for him to check a problem with the door lock. He looked at me skeptically and prompted me to tell him what else was wrong with the car. I insisted that was it. That's when he took me by the shoulders and turned me around to see my car in the service bay. He asked, "Don't you want us to fix that flat?" As it turned out, this was no slow leak but a gash in the sidewall, and I was clueless as to how long I had been driving in that condition. Sure I felt stupid, but it proved my point—"I know nothing about cars and I wish to know nothing about cars." Therefore, I am also quite bright to have found myself a husband-for-hire in this regard.

1085 Hickory Ridge Lane

I thought I was being a good mother. I thought I was helping my daughter Lisa through a rough time. I thought I was teaching her a lesson worth learning. I didn't realize that I was equally taking care of myself and learning the same lesson. I didn't realize that at all until I started to write this report and sob. This is the story of a house. The story began in 1981, when my now ex-husband and I took up residence in it. It continued in 1994, when we divorced and I moved out. It ended two weeks ago, when he and his second wife left it too, moving on to a new place.

Since Lisa lives half of her life with me and half of her life with her dad, this occurrence impacted her greatly. Unlike her brother and sister, who had already moved on to college dorms and then adult life, Lisa was still very much tied to that old family home of ours, the one that had been hers since birth. Therefore, she felt great emotions in the weeks leading up to the move. I tried to convince her that the anticipation of moving was worse than the reality would be, but she had difficulty believing me. Somewhere along the line, as we talked and talked and talked through all of the stages of her grief, we hit upon an idea that soothed her— after the house was emptied we would go there together to bid it a fond farewell.

I knew immediately what we would do there, the lesson I would teach. I would bring two old audiotapes that I had made and that she had never heard. One would be of her birth, the actual moment when she entered the world crying. The other would be a conversation I recorded with my dear departed bubbie in the last year of her life. I would also bring happy remnants of the past—Lisa's little baby booties, old photos, and the like—as I demonstrated to her that beginnings, endings, and everything in between are forever lodged in our memories, our hearts, our souls, and not in the physical locale in which they originally occurred.

As it turned out, the anticipation really was worse than the reality, and by the time Lisa, her dad, and stepmother actually vacated the house, Lisa was feeling fine and needed no closing ceremonies. But we had one just the same. In retrospect, I guess it was for my sake. Though I felt I had long ago broken that tie, said that goodbye, moved on, and even healed, I somehow needed to go there one last time, and so we did.

It was odd, but for the hour or two that we were in the house, we were strangely unemotional. We toured the place completely as I looked into every nook, cranny, drawer, closet, and cupboard. I was surprised, shocked, and pleased that "parts of me" still remained there: one window treatment, some of my original carpeting, most of my old light fixtures, and all my Formica countertops were still in place after twenty years. After the tour we settled in the room that had been Lisa's nursery, where we listened to and looked at all the things in my goody bag of portable memories. It was unplanned but impossible not to also reminisce about nursing her, rocking her, and singing to her in that room when she was a baby, impossible not to remember the white light that seemed to emanate from the wall, to bless us and keep us. But even after all the reminiscing, we did not cry. Instead, we posed for a few photographs and, without much fanfare, locked up the house and headed to a pizza parlor for dinner.

It wasn't until days later—as I sat writing of the experience—that an odd thought entered my mind and caused me to cry. With heart-crushing sadness I realized that one of my window treatments, some of my carpeting, most of my light fixtures, and all my Formica counters had outlasted love. And that's when I wrote down one more lesson for Lisa and for myself: some of those very portable memories in life can also be very sad. Therefore, it's OK to cry. Sobbing is allowed as well.

Goodbye, 1085. Thanks for the memories—the happy ones, the sad ones, and everything in between.

Dear Roberta

It is said that a woman is lucky if she has one true friend in life, and so by this definition, I am a lucky gal. But far beyond mere luck, I tend to think of myself as blessed, for I have Roberta in my life. My Yiddish dictionary tells me that the word for a female friend is *chaverteh*, and I love the rhyme, chaverteh Roberta, but even more, I love the woman herself.

"Bird" and I have been friends since first grade, and memories of our togetherness could fill pages. From elementary school, I remember birthday parties at her house and marching together in the Halloween parade, when I was a "sandwich man" and she a beautiful mermaid in a glittery gown. In junior high, I remember working on the school's literary magazine with her and performing in the chorus of musical productions in which she had the starring role. During high school, she continued to sing and act, while I helped her worry about the kiss she had to give her leading man in *Guys and Dolls*. We also worked on the

yearbook together and hung out at each other's hous-
es, where we did homework, discussed infinity, ate car-
ryout banana splits from Velvet Freeze, and earned my
father's nickname for us—the gigglers. Roberta is the
one who sang at my wedding and who helped me learn
to hum again after my divorce. And while we have
always been good friends, these years of facing the
world together as single women have bonded us in ways
that childhood experiences never could.

The most wonderful thing about Roberta is that she
is a good listener. When I am bewitched, bothered, and
bewildered, I talk to her. When I am *farmisht, baroygis,*
or *tsedrait,* I do the same. She knows everything there is
to know about my kids, my folks, and my career. She
knows more about my relationships with men than the
men do. She knows fully my fear of Mondays and
Januaries. And after listening to me since 1958, she still
continues to do so. Once, a man told me that the problem with me was that I had to tell each of my stories
twice. He was patently wrong. I don't have to tell my
stories twice; I have to tell them twenty times. The really amazing thing about Roberta is that she will listen
patiently and compassionately to each telling. This is a
gift beyond gold.

Roberta is also a terrific role model for me as a single woman. She has supported herself all of her adult
life, has always done meaningful work, and has always
been content on her own. Through her example, I
have learned that being on your own does not mean
being alone, as Roberta is a true and loyal friend to a
legion of people and a highly involved caregiver to her
eighty-six-year-old father and other family members.

Though she would be pleased for me if I were to find a man to love, she wants me to go it alone first so that I will know I can and so that I will choose a man from a position of strength and not from neediness. (And speaking of neediness, Bird completely understands my addiction to chocolate and bakes me the world's most delicious brownies.)

If all of this isn't enough to commend her to the Best Friend Hall of Fame, Roberta is also the greatest analgesic around. When the world hurts me, she is there to soothe my pain. In the early days of my divorce, I was going through a rough time. Feeling like a failure, I called the guy I was dating for a morale boost. I asked him to please say something positive about me. His response was that he'd need to think about it and get back to me! When Roberta heard this she was incensed. She sat right down and wrote me a beautiful letter outlining my virtues. Her "love letter" to me still hangs on the inside of my medicine cabinet, where I read it daily as I brush my teeth. And guess what—after all of these years, this is my letter in return.

Bird, when I use my fingers to count my blessings, you're there on the first hand. I love you dearly and can't imagine my world without you. Thank you for being in my life!

More Than Just Single

Connor is the three-year-old granddaughter of my friend Betty. Though smart and talented in many ways, this beautiful little girl was resistant to potty training. Thus it was just recently that she graduated to big-girl underpants. On the fourth morning of her new life, her mother asked which pair of pretty panties she wished to wear that day. Connor replied, "I don't think I want to do this every day."

I identified with Connor's remark, because there's something that I don't want to do daily either—I don't want to be single. No, no, don't get the wrong idea; I'm not saying that I am looking to get married. What I'm saying is that I'm sick of filtering every experience through the eyes of single-hood. In my case, I have an excuse—I write a weekly singles column. But oh what a lopsided view of the world this gives me and what a lopsided view of me this gives the world! Today I take the opportunity to remind myself—and my readers—that I am more than just single.

Gosh I liked that opening! The first paragraph provided a chuckle and the second one ended with an empowered little jab of the arm. I also had great plans for what I would write next. There would be three paragraphs, all of which started, "Yes, I think about men, but if you were to chop open my head what you'd really find there is . . ." In one of those paragraphs I would mention how full my life is with family and friends, in the second one I would talk about how fulfilling my career is, and in the last one I'd mention all the outside activities that give meaning to my life. The essay would close with a darling line—"Yes, I think about men, but that just comes with the territory when you wear the brand of big-girl underpants that single women wear. Thus I am comfortable with my interest in men, as long as it is in moderation and not my sole focus in life."

Oh wow, I was so proud of myself! What a nice message this was to pass on to other singles! I buzzed right along as I wrote a list of the oodles of people who fill my life. Moving on to my career as a motivational speaker, though, a strange thing happened—I began to stumble. After much reflection, I realized I am in a rut there. I love to give my programs but so detest soliciting new business that I have stopped doing so. Hmmm . . . Next, I moved along to a listing of my outside activities, at which time I came to a screeching halt.

I had been a member of Women Advocates for Divorce Education, but because of fights between our advocacy and educational arms, the group is now defunct. I had been a member of the Unicorners Square Dance Club, but because it was so painful to be passed around the square from man to man without having special feelings for any of them, I stopped dancing. I had been a member of a task force to reduce substance abuse at the college my middle child attended, but when she graduated, I ended my affiliation. I had been a student at Raymond Walters College, but the certification program I pursued did not fit my needs, so I quit. I could continue here, but I'm sure I've made my point. I should also mention that I don't play mahj, bridge, golf, or tennis. Hmmm . . . perhaps there's a problem here. Have I become lopsided?

OK, so my life boils down to hanging out with people—many of them men—and writing a singles column. Perhaps this is the occupational hazard of writing such a column, or perhaps all lives get out of balance when we forget to take inventory. Whatever the reason, I am thankful for this opportunity to review my life, and I plan to regrow my world in the days to come. I'm thinking of joining some new organizations. The Cincinnati Bicycle Club comes immediately to mind— I'll get a lot of exercise, be outdoors, and perhaps even meet a man or two. I didn't really say that, did I?

Glossary

Yiddish Word	Definition
baleboosteh:	an excellent and praiseworthy homemaker
baroygis:	angry, petulant
beshert:	fated
besherter:	destined one, soul mate, beloved
bissel:	little in quantity
bisseleh:	the diminutive of bissel
blintze:	a Jewish-style crepe—a pancake rolled around a filling, usually cottage cheese
boychik:	a little boy; an affectionate term for a boy or man (an Americanism)
brokheh:	a prayer of thanksgiving and praise, a blessing
bubbie:	grandmother
bubeleh:	endearing term for anyone you like, young or old

challah: an egg bread
chaverteh: the feminine form of the word
                     "friend"
chozzerai: junk food; food that is tasty but bad
                     for you
chutzpah: brazenness, gall
danken Got: thank God
daven: to pray (may be linked to the English
                     word "divine")
dumkop: a dumbbell, dunce
farmisht: mixed up emotionally, befuddled,
                     confused
farputzt: all dressed up, decorated
feh: a term of many meanings such as—
                     that's terrible, that stinks, phooey, I
                     hate that
forshpeiz: appetizers
fressing: to enjoy good food and drink—and
                     lots of it; to pig out
gai avek: go away
gantz: all
gedult: patience or stamina
geferlekh: awful
gehakteh tsores: literally this means chopped-up
                     troubles—when worries, troubles, or
                     woes go beyond the realm of the
                     ordinary, they are gehakteh
geharget: slain, or as mobsters would say,
                     "whacked"
gelt: money
genug iz
  genug: enough is enough

gerushah:	a rabbinic term for a divorced woman—a more Yiddish term would be ge-gete froi
glezel tai:	glass of tea
gornisht:	nothing
Got in himmel:	God in heaven! (an expression of frustration, anguish, or fear)
gotenyu:	an exclamation or anguished cry meaning dear God or oh God!
haimisher:	cozy, unpretentious, having the friendly characteristics that exist inside a happy home; considered to be a highly valued trait (this is the male version of the word; the female form is haimisheh)
hak mir a chainik:	make longwinded and annoying conversation; talk for the sake of talking
hoizen:	trousers, pants
hultie:	a person of loose morals; a debaucher
Ich vais:	I know
kasha:	like a rice pilaf but made with buckwheat groats
kibitzes:	to joke, fool around, wisecrack; socialize aimlessly
klutz:	ungraceful, awkward, clumsy person—a bungler
knishes:	a dumpling filled with potatoes or meat
kugel:	a casserole made of noodles
kumt arein:	come in

kvell:	to chortle with pride and glow with pleasure, to gush
kvetch:	complain
mach nacht:	literally, "to make night"; to go to bed or to call it a night
macher:	a big shot or big wheel (beware—if machers boast about their accomplishments, they become k'nockers, the derogatory sort of big shot)
machetunim:	relatives by marriage
maidel:	an unmarried girl; teenager
matzah:	unleavened bread
mavin:	an expert, a really knowledgeable person on a subject
mazik:	a clever, swift, or mischievous child, usually used in an admiring or doting manner
mees:	ugly
mensch:	an honorable, decent person who is totally trustworthy
meshugeh:	crazy
meshuggener:	a crazy person
mishpoche:	a family, including the most remote of kin
mit'n derinnen:	all at once, suddenly; a sudden or unexpected interruption
nafkeh:	whore
nebbish:	an innocuous, ineffectual, helpless, or hapless unfortunate; a sad sack, loser
nu:	though usually translated as "well" or "so," this word carries an implication of impatience or criticism

nu shoyn:	hurry up, do it now, do it already
ongeshtopt:	stuffed (may also be used as slang for very wealthy or stuffed with money)
oy gevalt:	a cry for help; a cry of fear or amazement
oy gevalt and geshrigen:	this is one step up from oy gevalt—it's not just a cry, it's a scream
patshke:	to fuss with or mess around with
pishke:	a little can or container kept in the home, usually in the kitchen, in which money to be donated to charity is accumulated
plotz:	burst, bust your guts
potch:	a slap or smack
rachmones:	pity, compassion, mercy
saichel:	common sense, good sense, good judgment
schnoz:	nose, from the German word for snout, "schnauze"
Shabbos:	the Sabbath
shadchen:	a marital matchmaker
shain:	beautiful or handsome
shanah-tovas:	Jewish New Year greeting cards
shandeh:	disgrace
shaygetz:	non-Jewish boy or man
shiksa:	non-Jewish girl or woman
shlemiel:	a simpleton, dolt, or foolish person
shlep:	to drag or pull, to move or perform slowly
shlimazel:	a born loser, someone for whom nothing seems to go right or turn out well

shlumper: a careless dresser or untidy person
shlumperdik: unkempt, sloppy
shmatte: rag
shmooze: to engage in and enjoy a heart-to-heart
                     talk, or friendly, aimless talk; chitchat
shnaps: brandy, whiskey, liquor
shoyn genug: that's enough already
shpilkes: extreme impatience, pins and needles
shrei gevalt: to shout in distress or amazement
shrei'en: to scream or shout
shvitz: to sweat
simcha: a joyous occasion
smetteneh: sour cream
takheh a
  metsieh: a real bargain (often said with sarcasm)
tochis: buttocks, behind, fanny
tsatske: a toy or inexpensive thing, also used as
                     a girl who fools around or lets men
                     take liberties
tsedrait: nutty, crazy
tsemisht: befuddled, mixed up
tsores: worries, problems, woes
umglick: a tragedy or great misfortune
vilde mensch: a wild person; deranged
vos iz dos?:   what is this?
yontifdik: a festivity, in a holiday mood
yortzeit: the anniversary of the day of someone's
                     death
zaftik: juicy, plump, buxom, well rounded
zei gezunt: be well—said in parting
zhlub: a coarse fellow, a slob